Amglish in, Like, Ten Easy Lessons

Amglish in, Like, Ten Easy Lessons

A Celebration of the New World Lingo

Arthur E. Rowse

with illustrations by
John Doherty

ROWMAN & LITTLEFIELD PUBLISHERS, INC.
Lanham • Boulder • New York • Toronto • Plymouth, UK

Published by Rowman & Littlefield Publishers, Inc.
A wholly owned subsidiary of
The Rowman & Littlefield Publishing Group, Inc.
4501 Forbes Boulevard, Suite 200, Lanham, Maryland 20706
http://www.rowmanlittlefield.com

Estover Road, Plymouth PL6 7PY, United Kingdom

Distributed by NATIONAL BOOK NETWORK

British Library Cataloguing in Publication Information Available

Library of Congress Cataloging-in-Publication Data

Rowse, Arthur E. (Arthur Edward)
  Amglish in, like, ten easy lessons : a celebration of the new world
lingo / Arthur E. Rowse ; with illustrations by John Doherty.
    p. cm.
  Includes index.
  ISBN 978-1-4422-1167-4 (pbk. : alk. paper) —
  ISBN 978-1-4422-1168-1 (electronic)
  1. English language—United States—Slang. 2. Americanisms.
I. Title.
  PE3729.U5R69 2011
  427'.973—dc23

                                                    2011022884

∞™ The paper used in this publication meets the minimum
requirements of American National Standard for Information
Sciences—Permanence of Paper for Printed Library Materials,
ANSI/NISO Z39.48-1992.

Printed in the United States of America

Contents

Preface

When I was growing up in Lexington, Massachusetts, in the 1920s, we had no "language arts" in my public grade school. We had separate classes in English grammar, spelling, and penmanship run by no-nonsense teachers. Despite having much difficulty twisting my wrist into the prescribed position for perfect penmanship in the Palmer style, I learned to love the language even with its many idiosyncrasies.

I liked to read books about boys going on great adventures and playing tricks on people. They made me want to write for fun or money. But since there were not many such paying jobs for ten-year-olds, I created my own job by starting a weekly neighborhood newspaper. I got the idea when my father gave me a cast-off Remington typewriter after I had spent a day "helping" him at his office.

My first brush with censorship came early when I put a snide dinner-table quip from my father into print. He had said a neighbor's new baby girl had been named "Hope" because the parents were hoping for a boy. My father made me run a crayon through the disputed sentence. I made sure the words remained visible. (The rebellious quality comes from living in "the birthplace of American liberty.")

My first bout with a stilted language came on graduation day after six grades at Hancock School when I was awarded a prize for scholastic excellence. I was hoping for something useful such as a chocolate cake, certainly not a copy of *Master Skylark, a Story of Shakespeare's Time*, published in 1897.

When I opened the book later and read the first page of flowery British prose by author John Bennett about "punts . . . poling slowly on the Avon" and "April sunlight dancing on the brazen horns and the silver bellies of the kettledrums," I put the book down for good. It was not my kind of English.

After four years as editor and publisher of the *Naborhood News*, I retired because of issues—today's in-word for such complications as schoolwork—that led to an editorial in the town weekly titled "Why Editors Quit." I eventually fell into some "higher education," World War II duty in North Africa and Italy, the authorship of a few books, and a string of editing and writing jobs mostly at Boston and Washington newspapers, where some knowledge of formal English was still required.

It wasn't until much later in life that I realized why my neighbors and relatives were willing to pay two pennies to read the *Naborhood News*. I concluded that it was not for the news, which was little more than a reflection of family dinner conversations. It was to laugh at all my malapropisms and mistakes in grammar and spelling. I remember one headline, BUM BITES GAS MAN, referring to a neighborhood dog.

By the time my own kids went to public school in Washington, D.C., in the 1960s, "language arts" were beginning to supplant the much-despised classes in grammar, spelling, and penmanship in some schools, though not yet in our neighborhood school. In fact, unknown to me at the time, the main English teachers' association of the country officially condemned separate classes in grammar in 1963, the all-time peak year for verbal SAT scores. I suspect that not many parents knew that "grammar" had become a dirty word.

In the next few decades, I became increasingly shocked at the failure of many Americans—at all levels of society—to absorb the basic fundamentals of their native language. My shock turned into disdain, especially for well-educated people who apparently didn't know the difference between *lay* and *lie*, *that* and *which*, and other fine points of proper English such as differentiating between subjective pronouns and objective ones.

But I had a linguistic epiphany after George W. Bush became president in 2000. Here was a budding world leader, a man of great privilege enhanced by education at prestigious schools, who appeared woefully unable to mouth a simple sentence without violating at least four or five basic precepts of English. At first, I marveled at how blasé Americans were about choosing a leader with such a gross deficiency in his mother tongue.

I joined millions of other people around the world snickering at the way the nation's most prominent bushwhacker shredded the language in such funny ways. It was during one of those laugh-ins I finally realized, languagewise, here was a politician who did not speak much differently from other Americans, including at times my friends, associates, and myself.

It also began to strike me that nobody can be a perfect master of English. Indeed, it is an impossibility because of the language's many mysteries and defects. We all make errors when using our native language, regardless of our education.

I began to realize that language errors have become an integral part of the current linguistic upheaval. Even more interesting are the many efforts to be original. New words and phrases are bubbling up at a furious pace, either by accident or design. And those who are not innovators help the process by passing along anything interesting that they encounter. The whole exercise is either a delight or a continuing disaster, depending on your point of view.

I chose the positive approach and became taken in by the charms of informal English, especially the neologisms, the grammatical variations, the innovative texting, the flood of acronyms, the smiley faces, and the disappearance of capital letters and punctuation. I also realized that there is nothing anyone can do to stop language from constantly changing.

The growing informality of American English mirrors what is happening to society itself. Just as most people are now choosing casual clothing, they are also becoming informal with language. It has become the in-way to bond with friends and associates while keeping pace with the latest trends.

I began to catch some of George W's joviality with language and to recognize the camaraderie and, yes, even excitement that goes with using language in new, more interesting, more enjoyable, more imaginative ways.

I also realized that it was no longer teachers and lexicographers who were shaping language. It was the great masses of ordinary people, especially young musicians, humorists, writers, and general dissidents who were leading the way. The process is a constant, natural churning that no language police or remedial teachers can alter.

Suddenly, it seems, almost everybody is speaking and writing more freely and enjoying it more. Many of the rules and standards that have served for more than four centuries are quietly being shelved as we speak and write. We are all constantly creating the new language that is Amglish, the title that some people have already given to it.

This is a momentous development at an exciting time. As if to prove the point, the top two editors of the popular online *Politico* reported in December 2010: "More traffic comes from an item on Sarah Palin's 'refudiate' . . . than from our hundreds of stories on the complexities of health care reform or Wall Street regulation."

Such massive attention to language change is unprecedented, and it's worldwide. The subject itself is so huge and so fluctuating that no book can do more than merely scratch the surface of the story. The field is wide open for further exploration.

While this book seeks to share the thrills of the emerging Amglish, it also recognizes the urgent need, especially for young people, to become proficient in their native language, whatever it is. The ultimate cool is knowing how and when to use the prevailing language of business and government for one's own benefit while fully enjoying the "current" wild world of informal language.

In order to paint a full and honest picture of today's language scene, I have let bits of Amglish fall naturally into parts of this book. My secret hope is that doing so will, like, give me immunity from any criticism about the way that, you know, the book is written.

Let the celebration begin.

Acknowledgments

FROM THE AUTHOR

A book like this one could not be done without the expert help and willing cooperation of many people, including some who are not aware of the roles they played in providing the evidence needed to illustrate the book's unassailable theses.

As the author, I would first like to credit my wife, Ruth Fort, for rekindling my interest in language with a book gift years ago relating to Sam Johnson's famous dictionary. I am deeply in debt to her for her unsurpassed editing and advice from the very beginning of this project. I am also grateful for her toleration of my single-minded devotion to an inanimate object for five years. I would like to put any gross errors on her shoulders, but that would be my first error.

Next, I would like to sincerely thank the world's greatest caricaturist, John Doherty, for his excellent work so prominent in these pages. John and I first collaborated in producing the famous Bush House of Cards in 2003. I also would like to thank his wife Judith for her extremely careful editing and generous advice.

I give special thanks to Niels Aaboe, Janice Braunstein, Sarah David, Matt Evans, Marissa Parks, and Sam Caggiula at Rowman & Littlefield Publishers for seeing the possibilities of such a book in the first place and for their advice and help since that momentous decision.

Still others who deserve very special mention include John Adams, Tony Badran, Carole Berke, Daniel Bouskela, Maria Angela Loquercio Bouskela, Feodor Bratenkov, Monique Briendwalker, Robert Chaddock, Margaret Chapin, David Crystal, George Dahl, Paul Dickson, Tsomo Faith, Adam Faulkner, John Fitzgerald, Jurgen Flach, Arthur Fort, Andrew Grant, Irene Grossman, Nick Grossman, Yi Han, Florence Lloyd, Charles Lund, Jay Matthews, Alexander Michaelson, Matthew Michaelson, Ahmed Moamber, Amal Mudallali, William Powers, Martha Rowse, Jim Roy, Julie Schoo, Molly Silvia, Denise Terry, Donald Terry, Tsemdo Thar, Serdar Tonbul, Larry Torres, Lowell Vizenor, Lawrence White, and Dario Zuddu.

FROM THE ILLUSTRATOR

One day in 2003, my phone rang and it was a man named Arthur Rowse proposing a collaboration on our project that became the Bush House of Cards. My response to him then was, "Boy, did you get the right number!" His vision on that project and on this book has been an inspiration to me. It's a great privilege to craft his ideas into visual form. His command of the language, his wit, and his ability to connect the dots sent me eagerly flying to the drawing board. So, thanks to him for making that call and for inviting me to share this work.

My greatest support and inspiration in my art and life is my wife, Judith Doherty. Her experience as a writer and editor added another set of eyes to this project, all the while juggling her own work and freelance schedule. And we stayed married! Thanks to Niels Aaboe, Sarah David, and all the staff at Rowman & Littlefield for their support.

Made in the U.S.A.

Peaceful Muslims, pls refudiate.

—Sarah Palin on Twitter, July 18, 2010

With her words above, the former Republican vice presidential nominee was trying to urge people to reject a proposed Muslim center two blocks from Ground Zero in New York City. She immediately drew some flak for partially misidentifying the issue and maligning Muslims. So she toned down the wording in a subsequent tweet.

But her worst crime, judging from press reaction, was to make up the term *refudiate*. Grammarians were shocked. Journalists exploded. "There's no such word," they shouted in print and on Twitter as they relished one more chance to show that the feisty former Alaska governor was out of touch with reality.

The flames temporarily singed Palin into hastily substituting the word *refute*. When that didn't work, she fired back, adding an old gem from former president George W. Bush and some slang for getting too excited:

"Refudiate, misunderestimate, wee-weed up. English is a living language. Shakespeare liked to coin words too. Got to celebrate it!"

Write on, Sarah! It's time to celebrate the new lingo that's sweeping around the world. All nitpickers should put their picks away. Let's face it, formal English is dying. A new, much less formal language is taking over this country and the world. And it's time to welcome it with open arms. In fact, there's no way to stop it.

IN PRAISE OF PALIN

Asher Smith, a reporter for the *Huffington Post*, was notable in his objection to the firing squad lined up against the former Alaska governor. "Hand it to Palin," he wrote. "Refudiate is catchy and sounds right to the ear." Smith had a point. Palin's word could be considered more logical than many words already accepted in the famously illogical English language.

What was so wrong about combining *refute* and *repudiate*? Palin had used the word a few days earlier on *The Sean Hannity Show* without arousing any reaction. Palin obviously assumed that was enough approval to make it an OK word in today's environment. She knew that the ultraconservative host would not allow a verbal abortion on his program.

And what about Palin's abbreviation for *please*? This slimmed-down version of the word was propelled by the advent of texting and has become so universally understood and accepted, especially on Facebook and Twitter, that none of her detractors even mentioned it. Language establishment leaders may not have been *plsd*, but they are no longer able to control the spelling of many *wds*, especially now that so many people are alluva twitter about language.

THE QUIRKS OF ENGLISH

For centuries, Americans have been trying to deal with the mysteries of the language their forebears heedlessly brought with them from England in the seventeenth century. No other language has ever been stitched together by so many sight-impaired, hearing-impaired, tongue-impaired babblers into such a crazy quilt of rules and traditions.

Numerous books, including many recent ones, have been written to show people how to comply with the increasingly outmoded requirements. Some sell well perhaps because of the large amount of grammar guilt still harbored by many people. But the only thing that has improved is the failure rate of national language tests.

What makes English so fascinating is not the impossible challenge of finding perfection so much as its large number of irregularities, defects, peculiarities, and just plain illogical requirements, not to mention the difficulties of pronouncing and spelling it.

People from all parts of society have tried to use their native language without error. But nobody has yet been able to do so, no matter how hard he or she or they have tried. There will always be some defect or quirk that prevents perfection. Take Mark Twain's words for it. When he considered the idea of English without error, he grunted, "The thing just can't be done."[1]

It should not be surprising that a new, less formal, easier-to-use version of English is rapidly taking shape with a character of its own. Among the names suggested for it, the best appears to be *Amglish*, since it is clearly an American version of English.

When Sarah popped up with *refudiate*, she—like countless lesser-knowns—was simply doing her bit to help the natural language process work its way. It was her explosive genius for mixing and matching words that captivated the public. Perhaps her most masterful coinage came on March 29, 2011, in the early phase of U.S. involvement in the Libyan uprising, when she was asked to assess the nation's role by Greta Van Susteren on Fox TV: "I too am not knowing. Do we use the term intervention, do we use war, do we use *squirmish*?"

No word, accidental or not, could better describe the American role after strongman Muammar Qaddafi refused to quit and the United States began efforts to unseat him without widening the conflict into a full-fledged war. Weren't many Americans squirming to find the right word to describe the situation?

COMMON SPEECH PATTERNS

It's not only Palin's uncanny ability to burst forth with the perfect new word but her concomitant ability to level with the average person by speaking in a natural, informal manner. She was in clover with Van Susteren, who has some similar language patterns.

For example, on the same show six days earlier, Van Susteren had asked her, "What do—what, in your opinion, is, in general, not necessarily just here, but the role of the military? Is—I mean, what—what is the role of the military?"

To which Palin replied: "Well, the UN obviously wants this—the role to be of our military just a humanitarian effort per the UN resolution that America has been a part of, and that's why we are engaged in enacting the no-fly zone. However, again, with Qaddafi having the blood of innocent Americans on his hands—and we have an opportunity to say, OK, finally we have—you're going to be held accountable. You're going to be gone."

Disjointed syntax like this, of course, is not unusual for ordinary conversations. But we used to expect leading figures and media types to use less fractured language on the public record. No longer. John McWhorter, a language specialist at the *New Republic*, saw a major change occurring when he wrote that "having trouble rubbing a noun and a verb together is not considered a mark against one as a figure of political authority."[2]

It should be clear to everyone by now: American English is rapidly changing into something much less formal when

WHAT IS AMGLISH?

It's informal American English, the first truly international tongue, the *lingua franca* for communicating between countries with native languages other than English.

It's also a tossed salad of new words, slang terms, tech talk, song lyrics, black talk, Valley girlisms, hippie speak, and hip-hop terms.

It's what some call nonstandard English, accidental words, "new" clichés, spoonerisms, malapropisms, misspellings, mispronunciations, and selective grammar.

It's acronyms, bureaucratese, Internet slang, tech talk, e-mailese, texting, instant messages, emoticons, and words mixed with numbers.

It's Bawlmorese, Bostonian, Brooklynese, Cajun, Chinook, Joysey, Looziana, Midwestern, Ozark, Philly talk, Texsun, WestVA, and other regional dialects.

And it's Arablish, Chinglish, Konglish, Spanglish, and dozens of other international mixtures called "lishes."

national leaders are catching the wave. It is pure Amglish. And it's bipartisan. All prominent politicians have misused their native language in one way or another. Vice President Biden has become famous for his "bloopers," one of which was his claim during the 2008 campaign that "the number one job facing the middle class [is] . . . a three-letter word: J-O-B-S." President Obama is also not immune to language slipups, as this chapter will make clear.

WHO SPEAKS AMGLISH?

All Americans speak Amglish whenever they depart—knowingly or unknowingly—from the rules of formal English or use words that are not in a standard dictionary. One departure doesn't make a new language, but a pattern of them is a good start. Even the best-educated people use Amglish to an increasing degree, often without realizing it.

There is no doubt that Standard English remains the prevailing language of business, government, and the media in the United States. But it is also clear from the many variations of it that the language is being transformed into something quite different from what it was only half a century or so ago.

Also changing in a big way is the ancient concept of language discipline. What matters now is no longer whether people speak or write correctly; it's whether they make sense and are understood, regardless of the rules or standards that are followed or not followed. As George Orwell observed, "Correct grammar and syntax [are] of no importance as long as one makes one's meaning clear." You can almost hear the amen chorus.

The groundswell toward less formal language is also being driven by the growing mix of the world's tongues in the United States and elsewhere. The crescendo of competing dialects and accents serves to further break down old barriers and install new, less confining ones. The numbers alone are impressive.

According to reliable British sources,[3] about 2 billion people speak some form of English, including about 500 million who grew up in an English-speaking household. The other 1.5 billion speak it as a second, third, or fourth language. Almost all these people speak an Amglish version of English.

If you take British author Robert McCrum's definition of "English speaking," the total number shoots up to 4 billion, more than half the earth's population of 7 billion, give or take a few hundred million. McCrum includes anyone having "knowledge of or acquaintance with some kind of English."[4]

With that definition, even a sheepherder in Nepal might know what to do if he and his flock came to a fork in the road with a signing saying STOP. But just as a few swallows don't make a summer, a few words don't make a person conversant in a language.

The British Council, a government-supported nonprofit with a mission to promote the language, estimates that by 2020, "nearly a third of the world's population will all [*sic*] be trying to learn English at the same time." That total might include the wordy writer of the prediction.

PALINISMS TURN GENERATIONAL

In response to some Facebook critics of the TLC reality show *Sarah Palin's Alaska* in November 2010, sixteen-year-old daughter Willow showed that she had learned Amglish well at her mother's knee.

After acronyming a few obscenities, she accused critics of being "jealous of my families [*sic*] success and you guys aren't goin [*sic*] anywhere with your lives." Her older sister Bristol added, "you're running your mouth just to talk sh-t."

After a brief session with Mama Grizzly, they apologized.

THE NEED FOR LEADERSHIP

As the third millennium neared, confusion over language standards was reaching a peak in the United States. English teachers appeared unable to explain why verbal SAT scores were dropping so steadily. And many students must have wondered why they were penalized for saying and writing things that were making equally young musicians and comedians filthy rich.

Older people who were not swept up by the new lingo probably wondered whether to ignore what they had learned in school or keep trying to conform while so many around them were not. And many young adults must have pondered when to follow the rules and when to run with the crowd. Everyone wanted to know how to act cool in the changing language environment.

Among those raising questions publicly was President George W. Bush when he asked, "Is our children learning?"[5]

Educators were shifting millions of students into remedial English courses without knowing how best to solve the plague of early dropouts from school. Many parents were also getting worried about whether their children's language was good enough for the job market.

The time seemed ripe for some kind of national language leadership. The basic question was whether formal American English was being—or should be—replaced and whether influential Americans should embrace the winds of change. A related question was who was going to step forward to help find the answers?

By the late 1980s, President George H. W. Bush had shown some awareness of the overall challenge when he offered up an occasional malapropism or grammatical lapse. At a formal dinner for the Pakistani prime minister on June 6, 1989, he admitted, "Fluency in English is something that I'm often not accused of."

But the next president, Bill Clinton, had too much love for formal English to lead a popular rebellion against it. His only public lapse came during a brief moment when he was questioned about the Monica Lewinsky matter, and he found it necessary to question the meaning of the word *is*. For this, he was sometimes called a cunning linguist.

JOY IN MUDDLEVILLE

The five-to-four Supreme Court decision in the contested election of George W. Bush as president in 2000—while ballots were still being counted in Florida—brought unbounded joy to the ranks of language rebels. Bush had clearly shown an intriguing originality with words during the campaign. He wasted no time connecting with the public mood when he blurted out, "They misunderestimated me," after his election.[6]

With those three words, George W. clearly signaled that he was primed for a leadership role in the language wars. Although he must have been exposed to some formal English at Andover and Yale, he obviously was more interested in things he didn't need lessons in, such as baseball and bar hopping. From watching his father, he also had become fully aware that a generous amount of broken English could bring handsome political rewards to men of privilege by leveling them linguistically with the hoi polloi.

However, his feisty mom presented a slight problem. Eleven years earlier, she had noticed a failure of many American families—possibly including her own—to be able to read and write English. So she formed the Barbara Bush Foundation for Family Literacy, no doubt to share the lessons that some in her own family had failed to learn at home with people who might better appreciate them.

In the end, she did not stand in George's way, and he was off and running. It was not until three years into his presidential term that he finally realized what his mom was so concerned about. He said, "The literary level of our children are appalling."[7] He were not joking.

AUSPICIOUS BEGINNINGS

Bush's knack for going with the flow of language was fortuitous for all Americans as well as for Amglish. Only three months after his inauguration, he saw the need to finally straighten out the long-standing public confusion over when to use the words *lay* and *lie*, just one of the language's many conundrums. Language authorities had tried for centuries to clear it up, but none had succeeded.

"We understand," he said, "where the power of this country lay. It lays in the hearts and souls of Americans. It must lay in our pocketbooks. It lays in the willingness for people to work hard. But as importantly, it lay in the fact that we've got citizens from all walks of life. . . ."[8]

The answer was finally clear: *Lay* is the choice, hands down, in all circumstances. End of problem. But a broader message was implied: that it was okay to wing it when faced with such quandaries in English, including when to use *who* or *whom*, *will* or *shall*, *that* or *which*, *further* or *farther*, et cetera. There has always been a leadership vacuum for such quandaries. Language authorities have never been able to explain them adequately.

When history finally assesses George W's deeds, lax lingo may be his greatest legacy.

WHAT IS IT ABOUT YALE AND LANGUAGE?

Students of Yale University tend to become either internationally famous for their language or hopeless followers.

Prominent in the first group, of course, are the two Bush presidents, lexicographer Noah Webster, and Dr. W. C. Minor, the convicted murderer who wrote much of the esteemed *Oxford English Dictionary* from an insane asylum, according to author Simon Winchester.[9]

Prominent in the second group is Bill Clinton, who uses formal English with scarcely a flaw. In a middling category are those who attended Yale but didn't graduate. Examples are Vice President Dan Quayle, whose main claim to fame was his imaginative spelling of *potato* when presiding at a student spelling bee, and former Veep Dick Cheney, who has done little to promote Amglish except mix up a few pronouns.

Even Jacob Weisberg, the journalist who exploited his famous fellow graduates with his *Bushisms* books, is a Yalie. Go figure.

NEOLOGISMS ARE US

At the same time, the country was becoming entranced with the idea of making up words and phrases as well as playing loose with grammar and syntax. It didn't matter whether the increasing laxness was accidental or purposeful. Language was becoming something to enjoy and be stylish with. Even the media, which have long prided itself by keeping up to the old rules, have joined the new game with vigor.

One of the more logical inventions is *idolspize*, a term promoted by the *Washington Post*—in a separate article—to denote simultaneously idolizing and despising a celebrity.[10] Just as one word can lead to another, so can one neologism lead to another.

A year later, the paper went into a full-page orgasm over the latest word for an important female body part, *vajayjay*. The term apparently got its start on ABC's *Grey's Anatomy* and then got massaged by Oprah and enough other TV personalities to gain entrance into Merriam-Webster's *Open Dictionary*. If the originating show had used the anatomical term instead, nobody would have noticed.

The *Post* chose to violate a famous language rule and use a noun instead of a verb to describe the way in which Hollywood's Joan Collins went "*swanning* through the lobby of the Ritz Carlton . . . with just the right accessories."[11]

Broadcasters can also play the game. NPR ran a contest to find the best neologism for an aborted sneeze. The witty winner was *sniff-hanger*.

ANCIENT NEOLOGISMS

Neologisms have been fun for centuries. One of the most fertile sources was Lewis Carroll, the author of *Alice in Wonder-*

land who also penned the delicious poem *Jabberwocky*, which still charms as much as it did in 1872. It is the source of our current word *chortle*. Carroll became an early supporter of less formal English, a thought that might cause him to chortle in his grave at the sight of it today. The first quatrain of *Jabberwocky* set the tone:

> 'Twas brillig, and the slithy toves
> Did gyre and gimble in the wabe:
> All mimsy were the borogoves,
> And the mome raths outgrabe.

The poem is a fine example of portmanteau words, those that combine at least two words. A common example is *smog* (*smoke* and *fog*). Carroll's *slithy* mixes *slimy* with *lithe*, and *mimsy* combines *miserable* and *flimsy*. It's the same game that Sarah played when she melded *skirmish* and *squirm*. Who doesn't enjoy this kind of wordplay?

Many neologisms simply appear and then hang around long enough to eventually become part of the linguistic woodwork. One of them is *nother*. No, that's not Old English for *mother*. It first got shrunk from *another* by Geoffrey Chaucer in the fourteenth century, but that's a whole nother story.

The rising tide of new words today raises an interesting question: are the media pushing them primarily to attract and hold their declining audiences or to put a pretty face on the new flexibility of their own standards? Or both? While the jury is out on that, a popular website, Urban Dictionary, has been busy collecting the verbal uppers and downers for all to admire and use. The result is a series of books of the same name. Sample entries: *sheeple* for people who are unable to think for themselves and *dot-gone* for an unsuccessful Internet company.

For eighteen years, the *Washington Post* has run a weekly contest called Style International in which entrants compete for prize T-shirts with humorous concoctions that often defy the laws of verbal gravity.

Dictionary publishers have also caught the bug with almost bizarre efforts to postpone their funeral. Merriam-Webster, for example, trumpets its "Word of the Day" based on voluntary offerings from inventive individuals. Like some competitors in the dictionary field, M-W seems to play the game more for attention than as a practical source of verbal definitions, now known as "defs," not to be confused with the hip-hop term for cool.

THE NEW NORMALCY

All these stirrings have made it abundantly clear that the language establishment has been losing its clout to prevent or control changes. Young people especially are learning how to shape language to their own tastes and desires. No longer are only a few wandering rappers and poets experimenting with new sounds and symbols. Everyone seems to be playing the game either by innovating or passing on what others invent.

As columnist Smith noted, Palin's neologisms immediately became part of "the new normalcy." By that he meant that she is not the one out of step; it's the parents, teachers, journalists, authors, and assorted nitpickers who still complain about what they see as misplaced apostrophes and butchered syntax.

Unlike traditional language leaders, Palin and Bush don't ride a high horse; they ride the power of example. Almost anything they—and other selfless pioneers—say reverberates throughout the world at Internet speeds. As a result, many words that used to be criticized—even shunned—are now readily accepted. And they quickly become part of a new pattern that is characterized more by disorder than order.

WHEN IS A WORD APPROVED?

It used to be the job of an important dictionary such as the *Oxford English Dictionary* to determine when a word is accepted into the English language. But no longer; that job has been claimed by the Global Language Monitor, a website based in Austin, Texas. It claims to have counted every word in the English language and at 10:22 a.m. on June 10, 2009, it declared *Web 2.0* as the millionth word.

But who's really counting, and what are the criteria? In fact, nobody knows how many words there are in the English language because there is no widely approved system of counting them. Nor does anyone know whether *Web 2.0* is a word or just a tennis ranking for a guy named Web. Tim Berners-Lee, the British inventor of the World Wide Web, calls *Web 2.0* "a piece of jargon." Actually, it refers to Web applications that facilitate interactivity on social media sites, not a second edition of the Web.

Trying to pin down such an amorphous mass of verbiage goes against the whole point of language today: to let human nature create the best way for people to communicate and understand each other.

In the new normalcy, it rarely makes sense to look up the meaning of a word in a dictionary. The unwritten rule seems to be, if you don't know the meaning, take a guess, because the word may be too new for permanent enshrinement, despite all the efforts of lexicographers to stay cool and relevant. Besides, who has the time for such details these days?

Much the same thing is happening to grammar and syntax. Even well-educated people are ignoring the old rules and making up their own. Traditional guardians of formal language, such as TV reporters and anchors, are increasingly letting words and phrases meander naturally. And daily newspapers are allowing more grammatical lapses, presumably while editors are out to lunch.

Not many people these days have the time for language details; they are often too busy phoning, texting, e-mailing, Googling, Facebooking, Twittering, YouTubing, surfing TV, or multitasking two or three activities at once.

For most people, especially younger ones, there's no going back to the picky past, with its stuffy rules and dying language. By accident or intelligent design, all of us are on the front lines of language evolution.

SNUCKERED AND DRUGGED

One increasingly popular word today never had legitimacy in educated circles. In the few cases where it was listed in a dictionary, it was dismissed as colloquial or worse. The word is *snuck*, now uniformly preferred over the prescribed word *sneaked* as the past tense of *sneak*. Like poetic fog on little cat feet, the word has moved stealthily into almost complete acceptance at all levels of society.

None other than Jonathan Yardley, a word master par excellence as the chief book reviewer of the *Washington Post*, let *snuck* sneak into his own prose in 2006.[12] His use of the term was a clear sign that the word had finally attained all the respectability it needed for today's atmosphere.

Once the dam holding *snuck* was broken, other journalists felt free to let it all hang out. One of the least likely copycats was *New York Times* columnist Maureen Dowd. She wrote a year later that she had *snuck* her sister into a press breakfast attended by President and Mrs. Bush in 2000.[13] The word was out: *snuck* had finally hit the big tent.

Another word on the way to respectability is *drug*, but not the medicinal or hallucinatory kind. This *drug* is posing as the past tense of *drag*. At least that is the way it was used on *BBC News* in 2007 by Ruth Wedgewood, a Johns Hopkins professor of international relations. During the scandal involving Paul Wolfowitz's tenure as World Bank president, she said his paramour had been "*drug* through the mud."

Shortly after Professor Wedgewood's courageous move, President Bush put the White House imprimatur on the word in discussing the long ordeal suffered by his attorney general, Alberto Gonzalez, in testifying before Congress about the firing of some U.S. attorneys. "This process," said Bush, "has been *drug* out a long time."

It means that Dizzy Dean, the famed baseball pitcher of the 1930s, did not labor in vain when he would say that a runner *slud* into third base. He also helped set a pattern for years to come with colloquialisms like "Me an' Paul (his brother Daffy) are *gonna* win forty-five games."

IT'S, LIKE, YOU KNOW

Two of the most common signs of Amglish are the terms *like* and *you know*, often uttered together unconsciously. One leader in this area is Caroline Kennedy, the daughter of the late President. In an interview with the *New York Daily News*, she bravely uttered "you know" more than 200 times, and during an interview with the *New York Times*, she did so an incredible 130 times according to a count by *Vanity Fair* columnist Christopher Hitchens.[14] The conversations were about the possibility of her running for the U.S. Senate. The possibility vanished, you know, after the interviews.

Language purists tend to look down their noses on such usage. But there is more here than meets the eye. To fully understand, you have to realize the fear and timidity that still grip many people, especially younger ones, as they try to conform to all the outmoded rules of formal English without appearing to do so.

In some cases, it might be an innate inability to speak with confidence. Quite a few people seem to need sentence fillers

to give themselves time to think through their options before speaking further. For them, words like *like* and *you know* are perfectly designed to provide those extra split seconds necessary to plan the rest of a sentence.

By public acclaim, *like* has also been pressed into service as an acceptable replacement for the antique conjunctions *as* and *such as*. So while some English teachers might still say a certain young man drove too fast "as he always has done," almost everybody else says, "like he always has."

Another relatively new use of *like* is to introduce a quotation or a separate clause. Michelle Rhee, the former chancellor of public schools in the District of Columbia, demonstrated

---

"BY THE WAY, HAVE A LOUSY DAY"

Nothing is untouched by the new lingo, including the routine way of parting after talking with another human being. What once was an upbeat *Good day* or *Good-bye* has turned into an entire sentence: "Have a good (nice) day," even when the speaker clearly has opposite thoughts.

Ginni Thomas, wife of the U.S. Supreme Court Justice Clarence Thomas, managed to set the gold standard for this sort of greeting in October 2010 when she called Anita Hill, a woman she hated for having testified against her husband's confirmation nineteen years earlier, to suggest that Hill apologize to him. She ended the phone message— at 7:30 a.m. on a Saturday—with, "Okay, have a good day."

Something similar occurs almost every time you finally reach a human voice after surviving a long "menu of options" on an 800 number and then are told—or you realize—that nothing can be done to resolve your problem, followed by the routine "Have a nice day."

More recently, this phrase has been reduced to "Have a good one," only to be topped by the caring TV anchor's "Have a great evening and a wonderful weekend."

such usage in the *Washington Post*. "When I joined Teach for America," she wrote, "my parents were like: 'What are you doing? Get a real job.'"[15]

Such use of *like* is further evidence of the fear and timidity gripping so many Americans when they are, like, speaking English. Like it or not, *like* and *you know* are here for the long haul.

Even the common verb *have done* now seems to be in play. For example, Jan Brewer, the governor of Arizona, was quoted in the news in 2010 using *have did* instead of *have done*.[16] To make sure that no grammar sticklers would accuse the reporter of such a verbal initiative, the paper inserted the Latin term *sic* to indicate what was actually said. That provoked one reader to ask why the same italic word was not used on the sports pages where athletes have did the same thing.

IS ANYBODY LISTENING?

One of the more versatile words is the simple adverb *hopefully*, which has become used most often as a conjunction. A typical example is, "Hopefully I'll see you when I get home." Grammarians have often objected for various reasons, but they have finally learned that "hopefully" springs eternal.

Even simple negatives can get lost if used too often. That's what seems to have happened to one of the more popular turnoffs, "I couldn't care less." For some reason, the more it's used, the less negative it becomes. Now, you are more likely to hear, "I *could* care less," just the opposite meaning. Yet nobody seems to notice that the revised phrase makes no sense.

Does this mean it's all right now to talk nonsense because nobody is listening? The answer must be yes if you believe, for example, that "drawing a line in the sand" is somehow an actual threat, as President George H. W. Bush famously did on November 17, 1991, when he used the phrase to threaten military action if Iraq's Saddam Hussein did not withdraw from Kuwait.

THE NEGATIVE TRIFECTA

Speaking of disposable negatives, the late Rodney Dangerfield made a lucrative career out of superfluous negatives, as illustrated by his theme, "I don't get no respect." Sometimes he would go for the negative trifecta by ending the phrase with "no how." Which raises the question: if two negatives make a positive, what do three create?

His accent on the negative had a positive effect on his career as a humorist. It also helped promote the copycat atmosphere of multiple negativity in the Amglish community.

Simply threatening to draw a line not to be crossed, of course, can be effective, but in the sand—where the next wave or puff of wind could wipe out the line? Not likely. Since then, the nonsensical cliché has proliferated with nary an objection up to the point where it is coming close to having no meaning at all, not because of its lack of logic but because of excessive repetition.

The sand metaphor refuses to fade away. At a press conference on Pearl Harbor Day, 2010, focusing on a tax cut deal with Republicans that few Democrats liked, a reporter asked President Obama, "Where is your line in the sand?" He responded, "Well, look, I've got a whole bunch of lines in the sand." For a brief moment, the emptiness of the phrase seemed apparent. But no, he started to draw a few more lines. Only in Amglish can such a contradiction gain immortality without a fight by the perfection police.

SELECTIVE GRAMMAR

A big key to the success of the new lingo is the natural inclination to follow the crowd rather than to question or doubt someone who is testing a new word or phrase. This has proven to be especially helpful in gaining acceptance for selective grammar. In the following sections on sentence structure and verbal moods, experimenting is in and conformity is out, even in high places.

Almost all the long-standing rules about sentence structure are losing favor. One is the increasingly mysterious relationship between subject and object, especially when pesky things like pronouns are involved. For example, many people simply dis the old rules about when to use the subjective *I* and the objective *me*.

There is a growing suspicion that the key to this is more a matter of dignity or politeness of the pronoun *I* than the grammar. Possibly for that reason, the sentence "He told Bob and me" may often come out, "He told Bob and I." However, if the same two people decide to do something together, the dignity factor may disappear, resulting in "Me and Bob will be going," possibly because "Bob and I" sounds stuffy.

This type of flexibility is being preferred at the highest levels. In a 2007 radio interview about the problems facing Attorney General Alberto Gonzalez, Vice President Dick Cheney referred to "the debate between he and the Senate." Cheney may have been trying to grab some of the linguistic fame of his boss, George W.

According to a survey of nearly 3,000 high school compositions in 1985, verb problems showed up nearly 6,000 times, or twice per paper, and pronoun problems occurred 3,000 times, or once per paper.[17] When problems become that big, they become *issues*, a term vaguely defined as two or more problems.

Suddenly, the idea that simple requests or even sincere *chancrous* can cause problems seems to have run rampant. (The previous word in italics was typed as the plural of *thank you* as one word but was automatically and irreversibly changed by my version of Microsoft Word.)

Since the composition study was done, the pronoun problem has been resolved by President Obama and his education secretary, Arne Duncan, by example. Obama is frequently shown on television at rallies saying, "You people were very kind [or gracious] to Michelle and I." In a televised discussion with Charlie Rose, Duncan obviously bowed to presidential precedence when he said, "The schools don't belong to you or I."[18]

These grammar patterns from on high should make it clear that the switch to less formal English is no longer confined to those with little education or station in life. They are rapidly becoming the pattern for all Americans. Grammar is coming down to a matter of personal choice.

2B OR NOT 2B?

Another dilemma that many older people believe is not a dilemma at all involves the most common verb, *to be*, along with its irregular and illogical forms, *am*, *is*, and *are*. Even Shakespeare recognized the problem when he had Hamlet say, "To be or not to be; that is the question." He was obviously asking why the simple word *be* cannot be used instead of all the irregular forms that complicate the verb so completely.

E. D. Hirsch Jr. is one noted author and educator who takes a realistic view of the issue. He has suggested that it would have been simpler to use *be* for all present-tense forms, such as *I be, you be, he be*, and so on. He says, "We don't need *am*, *is* and *are*. With English verbs, as with its pronouns, a single form can very well do the work of all, without ambiguity."[19] As for the chances of getting the language establishment to go along with that idea anytime soon, they be extremely small.

Meanwhile, slurred verbs like *wanna*, *gonna*, and *gotta* have long been on a tear, especially in newspaper headlines, often without quotation marks. My probes on Google in December 2010 showed the three verbal elisions catching up to their formal linguistic parents, *want to*, *going to*, and *got to*.

The most popular of the three was *gonna*, with 129 million hits. In comparison, the hits for *going to*, its formal equivalent, were 170 million. *Wanna*, the next most popular of the three, came in at 104 million, compared to 2.88 billion for *want to*. *Gotta* came in third with 65 million hits compared to 2 billion for *got to*. In another few years, the use of these verb forms may be gonna loosen up quite a lot more.

The slurring of words has a long tradition. Writing in the *New Yorker* in 1949, John Davenport said he coined the word *Slurvian* when he heard a person say she had just returned from a Yerpeen trip and had a nice time nittly.[20] Late-night comic Steve Allen took the Slurvian dialect even further with his phunny phonics, such as *widya* (why did you?) and *sokay* (it's all right). Such examples, however, are not pure Slurvian. To reach that rare status, a writer needs to make each slurred word another actual word, such as the following:

PURE SLURVIAN

We was at a bridge *torment* taking everything for *granite* with lots of other *lays in gems* when a woman in the *mill* of the big room yelled, "I think I've been robbed. Somebody call the *please.*" Just then, there was flashes of *lining* and strong *wins*. It was just like a *whore* story.

I asked to *bar* some snuff from the lady at *are* table who lives *next store* to us. She said *know* problem, then added, "*Less* calm down a bit . . . two many people have a *deep-seeded* fear of everything." I *greed* with her.

Inspired by Richard Lederer's *Anguished English*

At the same time, busy Americans like to add unnecessary words, thus increasing rather than decreasing their busyness.

The little word *at* has become very popular as an additive to a question about somebody's whereabouts. The question "Where are you?" brought 2.43 billion hits on Google, only slightly more than the 2.26 billion hits for the same question plus *at*. Leaving out the verb entirely, as in the common "Where you at?" yielded a respectable 1.86 billion responses.

Languagewise, this is where it's @.

WHAT'S A SUBJUNCTIVE, GRAMPA?

It's about time to say so long to subjunctives in almost every language. They are reminders of a much more ordered past when verbs denoting emotion, desire, or command required special care. Although the rules still require, for example, that you say, "If I were smarter, I would get better marks," even some language sticklers now tolerate *was* for *were*. President Obama for one.

At least the nation's top judge has endorsed the trend. Chief Justice John Roberts has taken a tentative stand against subjunctives, according to a news item in the *Washington Post*.[21] The paper quoted him as saying, "I mean, if it *was* an easy case, we wouldn't have it." He showed additional linguistic tolerance by omitting the word *had* before the last *it*. But who's watching? Or listening?

Thankfully, speakers of Amglish don't need to worry about such things. They don't bother with subjunctive or pronoun rules. They know there are not enough language police with the lung power to blow the whistle if such a rule is not followed. Indeed, some teachers may be willing to show you how to get around such problems. For example, instead of saying, "If I were you, I'd be quiet," you could simply say, "Shut up."

LET YOUR FINGERS DO THE TALKING

No book about American language would be complete without a section on the latest advances in finger lingo, otherwise known as gesturing—of course in the informal spirit of Amglish.

Although the gentle fist bump was used occasionally before 2008, it did not reach wide acceptance until Barack Obama used it during the campaign and to celebrate his election with his wife, Michelle, before the TV cameras and the vast crowd in Chicago. Since then, it has come close to replacing the high-five slap of open palms to celebrate any kind of victory.

Meanwhile, the thumbs-up signal has gained ground over an ordinary smile to mark even a small victory where there is nobody to bump fists with. Likewise, the thumbs-down sign is fast gaining ground as the second most favorite signal for disapproving of almost anything.

But nothing can replace the third finger for expressing extreme disapproval or contempt. Former White House aide Rahm Emanuel became the poster child for this digit when he apparently used it once too often and had the end cut off by accident. Most people now reserve the universally recognized put-down for vexing traffic situations.

Also becoming extinct are adverbs, those mysterious things designed to modify verbs. Although an adverb is usually easy to form by adding an *-ly* to the adjective form of the word, few people have the time to add the two letters. Nor do many people have the time for a full verb in the common greeting, "How ya doin'?" And when it comes to a response, it's usually "I'm good," even though the responder is not and never has been a do-gooder and probably never done good in school either.

Signs of this trend dot the nation's roads and highways. An example is the warning DRIVE SAFE. It's enough to still cause some educators to take offense. But that might not include Jerry

Weast, a former Maryland school superintendent, who was quoted by a reporter as warning students to "drive careful."

CREATIVE SPELLMANSHIP

One of the strong attractions of Amglish is the absence of spelling rules except the one to write generally the way a word sounds. The only problem with that is the large number of words with the same interior spelling but different sounds. Examples are *bough*, *cough*, *though*, *tough*, and *through*. Computer spelling apps can sometimes help, but they are far from perfect as this anonymous ditty attests:

Eye have run this poem threw it
I am shore your pleased two no
Its letter perfect in its weigh
My checker tolled me sew

Another alternative, of course, is to look up a word in a dictionary. But that can be another time waster. If spelling is still a problem for you, you might consider moving to a country like Italy, where there is no such thing as a spelling problem. Each letter is supposed to be pronounced the way it is written. The only complication is the large number of words that sound exactly the same but have different meanings.

If you can't or won't move to Italy, you might wing it the way one eighteen-year-old graduating senior did in the following e-mail to her teacher in pure Amglish. By June 2008, she had been admitted to college from a charter school in the District of Columbia. Here are excerpts as written:

i have 2 take summa skol for English and a lil bit of math (i kno but i spoke to [name omitted] about it and i wil let her kno about how my schedule will run. . . . i need 2 meet up wit you cuz i need sum help on finaical part ther gave me . . . maybe saturaday or Sunday.[22]

At least the message was clear enough, so who can say Amglish doesn't work?

THE QUAINT ART OF PENMANSHIP

In the National Museum of Language in College Park, Maryland, cursive handwriting has an honored place amid the coffins for adverbs and subjunctives. In the dark ages, it was still commonly taught. But it's rare now. This antique style was replaced long ago by the "QWERTY" keyboard, first on typewriters, then on computers.

Emerging in its place has been a type of creative manual printing in a style that is original with each person. But who needs even that anymore? It is getting rare for anything to be handwritten except grocery lists and some phone messages. Meanwhile, the average scribble has now been upgraded to "cursive printing."

Yet some English professors keep trying to fight the odds. One is Tina Blue, who posted a complaint on the Internet saying she was "about ready to throw in the towel" because she could no longer read or understand many of the student papers she received in her work. So she conducted an experiment that forced her students to copy numerous printed articles by hand as rapidly as possible. Behold, their penmanship improved noticeably. So all she needs to do now is take away their phones and laptops and make them write by hand.[23]

Fat chance.

PANDAS AND PUNCTUATION

Those little squiggly things that used to be important points of pause in good writing are suffering the same fate as adverbs and subjunctives. They are increasingly ignored. They are also becoming impractical for today's busiest communicators. Try using them in a text or a tweet of 140 letters or less.

You cant.

A major attempt to save these picayunities came in 2003 in the form of a runaway best seller called *Eats, Shoots & Leaves* by a nitpicking British schoolmarm named Lynne Truss. The book offers several pages of panda stickers as rewards for good punctuation. Among Truss's most vulnerable targets are dirt farmers in her neighborhood who fail to use apostrophes properly on homemade signs selling fruits and vegetables.

She uses more than two hundred pages of text to advocate for more and better punctuation even while admitting that "modern technological communication threatens to wipe out the subtleties of punctuation altogether."[24] Apparently trying unconsciously to prove her last point, she gets caught advocating more punctuation than her own sample sentences can decently bear.

She is also just plain wrong in many areas, according to Louis Menand. The Pulitzer Prize–winning author found many misplaced commas, semicolons, apostrophes, and parentheses, plus a failure to adjust the book's style to an American audience unfamiliar with British punctuation style.[25]

If an expert on punctuation can't do any better than that, perhaps the answer is to omit all kinds of marks, period. That might satisfy all the buyers of her book who expected stories about pandas.

AN ARMY OF CURMUDGEONS

Truss is merely one of many curmudgeons who have been fighting a rear-guard action even while losing the war to retain formal English pretty much as it always has been. Their weapons of choice in recent years have been books with cutesy titles but questionable purposes. Truss's subtitle reveals her grim and unrealistic aim: *The Zero Tolerance Approach to Punctuation*. For this, she is now worth millions.

Among similar titles published since her 2003 bestseller are *Between You and I*; *A Little Book of Bad English*; *Grammar Snobs Are Great Big Meanies*; *The Gremlins of Grammar*; *Woe Is I*; and

When You Catch an Adjective, Kill It. Despite the cleverness of these titles and many others like them, informal English keeps picking up speed, leveling almost all roadblocks and bumps along the way.

The strained humor of these books shields their main purpose: to mercilessly exploit the average person's hidden shame that they can't handle their own language any better than they do. Rare is the native speaker of formal English who has complete confidence when speaking or writing.

Books may not be the ideal way of communicating with people who want to get better at punctuating sentences. A survey done for an independent publishing service showed that 42 percent of college graduates never read another book after college.[26]

THE SIGNS OF CHANGE

Long-standing rules and traditions are being increasingly ignored by all levels of society. Among the fading commandments are these:

- Thou shalt not make a sentence without a subject, object, and verb.
- Thou shalt not make verbs out of nouns.
- Thou shalt modify verbs with adverbs, not adjectives.
- Thou shalt use the subjunctive form of verbs when referring to conditional or emotional situations.
- Thou shalt not use *like* and *you know* as meaningless conversation fillers.
- Thou shalt not refer back to a singular subject of a sentence with a plural pronoun, such as saying "anyone can go their own way."

- Thou shalt not use the word *like* for *such as*, like in this sentence.
- Thou shalt use a possessive, not objective, pronoun with a verb ending in *-ing*, such as saying "he didn't mind *their* going," rather than *them* going.
- Thou shalt not put subjects of sentences in the objective case, such as "Bob and me went to the store"
- Thou shalt not use the word *be* for irregular forms of the verb *to be* in the present tense, such as saying "I be going."
- Thou shalt not excessively use abbreviations or acronyms.
- Thou shalt spell words correctly no matter what spell-check or your inner soul says.
- Thou shalt not elide verb forms such as *going to* and *want to* into *gonna* and *wanna*, no matter how much you *wanna*.
- Thou shalt always punctuate, and pronounce, words correctly.
- Thou shalt not use words not heritaged in the *Oxford English Dictionary*.

If you add all these and other rule changes to the unprecedented flow of new words, it becomes clear that a new version of English is being constructed as we speak and write. It is still basically English, of course, but it is taking on a character of its own as it reshapes itself to fit the changes in society.

LITERACY AND LANGUAGE

As adults become less able or willing to use formal language, their children are likely to care less about learning the rules. The trend is clearly toward less formal language and lower public literacy. But definitions of literacy are slippery.

If it is defined as being able to understand written text and participate in society, U.S. fifteen-year-olds are about average, according to an international assessment of literacy in 2009 by the National Center for Education Statistics. It showed that 30 percent of young Americans reached "proficiency" level 4, while 18 percent fell below level 2, "a baseline of proficiency." The results put U.S. participants in fourteenth place among thirty-four countries in the survey, about where they were in 2000.[27]

According to a survey by the U.S. Department of Education in 2008, roughly 40 percent of Americans of all ages scored at either the basic or below-basic level of proficiency in English. This meant that two out of five adults knew so little about formal English that they could not write a simple letter about a billing error.

A what? Who writes letters anymore? Can you remember the last time you wrote a complaint letter and actually mailed it? Just think of all the energy and time that goes into the process: the typing (hand printing?), folding, inserting it in an envelope, sealing the envelope, attaching the proper stamp, addressing the envelope, adding the return address, and dropping it in the mailbox for anytime delivery. The exercise is called snail mail because it's not only slow but for the birds. Of course, going through an automated telephone menu is not fast either.

It might be more in line with today's customs for researchers to assess the ability to text or telephone while multitasking, two more prevalent means of communication today. The figures might show much more functional literacy than old-fashioned assessments do.

EARLY PIONEERS

Alteration of the language inherited from Britain began as soon as the colonists hit the beach. H. L. Mencken, who chronicled many of the early changes in English in this country in his mammoth book *The American Language,* says the colonists eagerly explored language changes and "freely exchanged parts of speech, turning verbs into nouns, nouns into verbs, and adjectives into either or both with an abandon that is still one of the hallmarks of American English."[28]

There was also a continuous free exchange of language between the colonists and the natives. The power of guns over darts and arrows forced the natives to pick up the invaders' language in a heap big hurry. The exchange of words gave the resulting mishmash a decidedly Native American flavor.

Mencken called the mixture "American" to distinguish it from British English, which many intellectual Americans have tried to preserve over the years despite a largely libertarian climate. Indian terms that survive include *chipmunk, hickory, moccasin, possum, pecan, podunk, powwow, raccoon, skunk, squash, toboggan, and woodchuck.* Most come from the Algonquin tribe since it was the one most closely in contact with early English settlements in the eastern part of the country.

Today's Americans can't go far without running into Indian place names. They include half the states and hundreds of communities, such as Chicago (Algonquin for "garlic field"), Manhattan ("island" in Algonquin), Milwaukee ("good spot" in Algonquin), and Pensacola ("hair people" in Choctaw). Then there are Massachusetts places that sound like a lunch menu: Mashpee, Chicopee, and Sippewisset. Or is that a bus line?

Many native languages are still spoken. One of them is Navajo, which earned a special place for itself with the Marines in World War II. Without any alphabet or symbols, it proved ideal as a code that can't easily be deciphered. For starters, consider its equivalent of the word *navy*: "tsah wol-la-chee ah-keh-di-glini tsah-ah-dzoh." Another Indian language, Choctaw, served the same purpose in World War I.

ASIAN CONNECTIONS

Little noticed was the ability of many Indian tribes to understand each other, a fact indicating that their languages had a common Asian connection. According to the Smithsonian Institution, Siberian ancestors of American Indians crossed the Aleutian chain by dogsled about 14,000 years ago when sea levels were some three hundred feet below present levels. They then spread throughout the Western Hemisphere.

An Asian flavor can easily be detected in many Indian words and phrases, as well as in the names of the tribes themselves, everywhere from Alaska to Brazil. Verbal likenesses include *tangwaci* and *mamaci* ("father" and "mother") in Southern Paiute, and the words for "two" and "three" in Innu (related to Algonquin), *nishu* and *nishtu*. To eat in Innu is *mitshu*.

A YANGTZE DOODLE?

Even the familiar Dutch-American term *Yankee* may have partly originated in the plains of Asia, according to an item in H. L. Mencken's *The American Language*.[29] It says the word may be from the Persian *janghe* or *jenghe*, meaning a warlike leader. So does that make the terrible Genghis Khan the first Yankee Doodle Dandy?

Say it ain't so.

According to Polat Kaya, a former Turkish government official and researcher for Bell-Northern Research in Ontario, there are numerous similarities between Indian words and Turkish ones.[30] He claims that ancestors of Turks and others shared central and northern Asia with ancestors of American Indians. Kaya adds that many ethnic Turks still live in Siberia up to the Kara Sea and the Bering Strait, as well as in central Asia, illustrating the broad sweep of Turkish influence.

His comparison of the words for father (*ata, apa, baba*) in Turkish with forty-seven American Indian languages shows many similarities. Close parallels to the Turkish words for father include *atataq* in Eskimo, *adaq* in Aleut, *atotuh* in Cherokee, *tatag* in Algonquin, *ta* in Navaho, and *apa* in various South American tribes. The Turkish words for mother (*ana, anne*) also have many Indian likenesses, according to his research.

Today's lingo, of course, also contains flotsam from the early arriving Spanish, French, Dutch, and Germans, as well as others. Words include *crevasse, carryall, prairie,* and *-ville,* the suffix to many place names, from the French; *banana, cockroach, lasso, corral, mosquito,* and *ranch* from the Spanish; *boss, pie, stoop,* and *spook* from the Dutch; *noodles* and *sauerkraut* from the Germans; *goober* (peanut), *gumbo* (soup), and *hoodoo* from African slaves; and *butternut, bullfrog, eelgrass,* and *lightning bug* from the English.

This chapter has described how Amglish is becoming the common language of the United States. The next chapter will tell about how teachers, musicians, poets, comedians, advertisers, and others have unconsciously prepared the new language for shipment to the rest of the world.

Teachers and Other Pioneers

The teaching of formal grammar has a negligible . . . even harmful effect on the improvement of writing.

—The National Council of Teachers of English, 1963

The national swing toward Amglish is due to many factors, particularly the dedicated work of groups and individuals who see a future for less formal language.

Among the groups, none has been more supportive than the leading organizations of English teachers in the United States. With the awkwardly worded sentence above, the National Council made clear that it knew nearly half a century ago which way the linguistic wind was blowing, and it wasn't toward more formal instruction.[1]

Bravely reversing 2,500 years of grammar tradition, the group claimed "in strong and unqualified terms" to have "about a century of research" to back up its theory that the best way to teach grammar is not in a separate class devoted to it but only incidentally to teaching reading and writing.

Since then, the NCTE, which says it has about 60,000 K–12 English teachers as members, plus some 500,000 users of its website, has issued further resolutions firmly backing its 1963 policy statement. Most teachers have gone along with the council's initiatives.

CITING STUDENT RIGHTS

Moving in the same direction as the teachers—but with an intriguing twist—has been the Conference on College Composition and Communication (CCCC), which shares the same office building in Urbana, Illinois. Representing mostly college English instructors, the Conference determined in 1974 that students have the right to speak and write virtually any way they want—whether in Spanglish, Ebonics, Valspeak, or Geekish—and teachers should respect that right. The official statement said,

> We affirm the students' right to their own patterns and varieties of language. . . . The claim that any one dialect is unacceptable amounts to an attempt of one social group to exert its dominance over another. Such a claim leads to false advice for speakers and writers, and immoral advice for humans.

In other words, what could be called a mistake in formal English could mean a dialect that needs protection, not correction. The wording reflected the difficulty English instructors themselves were having reconciling the demands of teaching with the need to be politically correct. The instructors obviously chose the latter, and the cause of promoting less formal English has benefited as a result.

As if to demonstrate the difficulty of being grammatically and politically correct at the same time, the Conference delegates spent most of one day's session arguing over whether to use the singular word *student* which would trigger the awkward but PC words *his or her* as the later references. They chose to fudge the issue by using the plural.

Since then, the language establishment has quietly found it necessary to bend the old grammatical rule and allow the plural word *their* to refer to a singular collective noun such as *whoever* or *anyone*. However, language authorities have never officially acknowledged their rule change, which trailed the decision of the general public by decades.

DIALECTS ARE US

The Conference seemed to be saying that all students have a right to speak and write the way they want, and teachers should not try to correct them for fear of imparting "false" or "immoral" advice. In other words, "dialects are us," and young Americans from all backgrounds are the beneficiaries.

The Conference went even further by issuing a background document saying in part, "If we can convince our students that spelling, punctuation and usage are less important than content, we have removed a major obstacle in their developing the ability to write."

NCTE officials have heartily backed the Conference's stand on these matters. Randy Bomer, director of language and literacy studies at the University of Texas and a former president of the Council, told me, "Students have the right to remain attached to and use language they are comfortable with. We need to respect the languages that kids bring to school."[2]

But what is "content"? Nowhere in the websites of the two teacher groups is there a simple, easily accessible definition of the word. The vagueness of such a key term is another sign that educators are doing their part to encourage more informal English. They make that clear by saying that spelling, punctuation, and how you use the language are not as important as what you say and what the message is.

In other words, the old-fashioned concept of "correctness" in language is no longer as important as the ability to get another person's attention and understanding. If your grammar is iffy, your spelling is nothing to brag about, and you sometimes use a wrong verb tense or pronoun, yet other people know what you mean, what's the problem? After all, isn't being able to communicate the ultimate purpose of language?

The teachers could not be clearer in their endorsement of informal English. It fits today's attitude of many students who like to mock or ridicule those who get good marks and try to use formal English. In effect, both students and teachers, along with many others, agree that informal English is the way to go.

As *Washington Post* media critic Tom Shales wrote in 2007, "Being well-schooled, well-trained and experienced is actually acquiring a taint." A popular bumper sticker at the time of the teachers' shift in views said QUESTION AUTHORITY. It simply means that society and language have been changing together.

Even the word "English" has become too scary for the youngest of learners. As a subject, it is now almost universally called "language arts" or "language studies." And "grammar" has become such a dirty word that it hasn't been used to name an elementary school in half a century or so.

FOOD FOR CRITICS

Few people outside the education community got any inkling of this huge shift in policy. It was barely noticed by the mass media. But it aroused a few harsh critics. Former NBC newsman Edwin Newman was among the more prominent. In a 1974 book, *Strictly Speaking: Will America Be the Death of English?* he answered his own question with an emphatic yes.[3]

Needless to say, many Britons also have been deeply disturbed by what they see as a coarsening of English by the Americans. In 1995, the Prince of Wales complained that the U.S. version was "corrupting" the Queen's English. He said Americans "tend to invent all sorts of nouns and verbs and make words that shouldn't be." He added that "we must act now to insure [*sic*] that . . . English English maintains its position as the world language well into the next century."[4] He didn't realize that this Battle of Britain was already lost.

PISS ENTERS THE ROYAL CHAMBER

Prince William, the son of the Prince of Wales, seems to be setting a language tone more toward Amglish than his father might like. In January 2010, he was asked about his musical preferences while greeting a crowd of well-wishers in Australia. He blurted out, "I normally get the piss taken out of me for my choice of music. Bit rappy."[5]

Others who have resisted the trends include David Mulroy, a language professor at the University of Wisconsin. He attacked the NCTE policy on grammar in a book entitled *The War against Grammar*.[6] In it he said, "It is hard to give any kind of language instruction to students who lack the conceptual framework provided by the terms of basic grammar." He added that inserting some grammar into other parts of a school curriculum "is like trying to insert partial foundations beneath half-finished houses and concluding from the ensuing debacles that foundations are useless."

It is telling that Mulroy had to reach back to the ancient Greeks to find a society that really revered grammar, which eventually became the first of the seven so-called liberal arts. Since then, the enamor for grammar has been on a downhill slide all the way to today's U.S. society.

THE CURMUDGEON IMAGE

Did the NCTE's decision to relax grammar instruction have anything to do with the desire of English teachers to wipe out their traditional image as curmudgeons ready to chastise a weak student in front of others?

Former NCTE president Randy Bomer acknowledged the possibility by officially denying it when he declared that English teachers "do not see themselves as grammar police, on the lookout for mistakes and intolerant of diverse ways of speaking." But even in a writing class, a teacher cannot help becoming an enforcer when correcting a student's speech or prose in the presence of other students. After all, what is a teacher who doesn't teach?

FALLING TEST SCORES

The steady relaxation of formal language standards may have had an effect over the years on test results from the College Board's annual Scholastic Aptitude Test (SAT) for verbal skills. But the Board has done its best to cover up the actual scores. Apparently that is its way to go with the flow. (The Board refused to honor several phone and e-mail requests from me for scores back to 1963, but I obtained them elsewhere.)

The Board has even gone so far as to fudge its own figures. If you had followed its news releases since 1994, the important average score for the verbal part of the annual test went up from 478 in 1963, the year of the NCTE's big shift on grammar, to 501 in 2010.

But the scores actually went down. The 2010 score does not show what happened in 1994, when the total had plummeted from 478 in 1963 to 419. At that point, the Board figured out how to make things look better. It added 80 points to the scores. It explained that the test needed to be "recentered" to reflect a study indicating that the decline was largely due to an influx of poor blacks and Hispanics during those years.

So if you subtract the 80 points from the 2010 score, you get a substantial decline from 478 to 420 over the fifty-seven-year period. Meanwhile, the Board has inflated the scores from before the "recentering" of the SAT, which it previously called "an unchanging standard." Even the middle name of the test has been changed from *Aptitude* to *Achievement*, apparently to make it go down better.

As to the reasons for such poor student performance on the tests, the Board had a basketful of possibilities beyond those already cited, including changes in the national culture, lower scholastic expectations, a proliferation of nonacademic courses, and less homework.

But a Cornell professor contended that the overall decline was more likely caused by a sweeping simplification of schoolbooks over the earlier years.[7] Donald Hayes said the idea was to describe more common experiences so that children could read and learn the language more easily. "But," he added, "if you simplify texts, you deprive children of concepts associated with uncommon words."

A PRINCIPAL ON THE FRONT LINES

Parents of students at the Middle School of Art and Philosophy in New York City got another type of clue as to why SAT verbal scores have dropped so much: an e-mail from Principal Andrew Buck in 2010 defending his attitude toward education.

It contained some imaginative uses of pronouns, syntax, and other signs of informal English. Parents had objected earlier to the lack of what they felt were sufficient textbooks. Now they wondered whether the principal himself knew formal English. He obviously was trying in his own way to prepare his students for the changes in social and linguistic standards that had occurred since the complaining parents had gone to school.

A sample sentence of his: "Text books are the *soup de jour*, the *sine qua non*, the nut and bolts of teaching and learning in high school and college so to speak."[8]

MORE GRAMMAR SLAMMERS?

The war against formal grammar finally reached teachers of English as a foreign language (TEFL) in 2005, when they began considering whether to discontinue teaching the subject in their English classes. A British government study covering one hundred years of grammar research had concluded in January of that year—nearly half a century after the NCTE decision—that such classes did nothing to help students write more accurately or fluently.

The prospect of such a move inspired Luke Meddings, a British author and teacher, to comment in the London *Guardian*, "Grammar is becoming a sort of touchstone for our atomized 21st century souls. As we contemplate the end of civilization as we know it, without having really mastered it in the first place, it speaks to us of order and control." He also offered some words from Geoff Barton, head teacher at King Edward VI School in Southampton: "There may be no evidence that grammar teaching has improved writing, but . . . no conclusive evidence that it hasn't."[9]

MAJORING IN REMEDIAL

Of far more concern than punctuation and grammar are the growing dropout rates in high schools, especially where black and Hispanic students predominate. The rates are often double the national average, which hovers around 30 percent. At some colleges, up to 80 percent of incoming freshmen wind up in remedial English classes despite the fact that almost all colleges have been forced to lower their standards to remain competitive in the market for students.

In an effort to improve student language skills, the educational establishment has intensified remedial courses that seem to be geared to a long-past era, one that English teachers themselves rejected long ago. The idea is apparently to pound outdated English rules and exceptions into increasingly less formal and more rebellious students in a decreasingly formal social environment.

While formal English is being increasingly rejected by the population as a whole, remedial classes to support it have proliferated. As a result, many students essentially major in the subject to the exclusion of a broader education.

Although remedial teachers may be able to claim some improvements in test scores, the overall experience may be souring students by the millions on learning the standard language, while they frolic outside the classroom in an atmosphere where virtually the only learning comes from fun and games.

The plight of one remedial student illustrates the dilemma. The following Amglish was posted on *Yahoo! Answers* by a student calling himself Jason:

> I can't pass remedial english class? this is my third time taking it finally i have passed to the 2nd semester of it but i'm burnt out. im doing good on everything besides English and i have heard that college level English classes 101 and 1A are way easier than remedial English class. can someone help me out i don't know what to do[10]

Remedial English courses are even beginning to become explosive. A "civil war" broke out in 2010 at City College of San Francisco (CCSF), when a college trustee suggested that such classes be limited to one year instead of being required for as many as five semesters. Approximately 90 percent of the 100,000 students at CCSF are not considered ready for introductory English 1A. As a result of the furor, CCSF chancellor Don Q. Griffin decided to shorten the remedial courses.

CALLING ALL INNOVATORS

My review of research papers on remedial English courses shows virtually no effort to examine their relevance to the vast bulk of young people today. Nor does there appear to be any rush to devise new ways to teach English in such changing conditions.

A major review of the situation by the University of Massachusetts in August 2010 confirmed that American educators appear to have reached a dead end in efforts to bring all students up to speed for today's IT world.[11] Even the experts who wrote the report showed their secret affection for Amglish by by committing a few glaring grammatical errors.

The bottom line is that Amglish is winning the language war. It is incumbent on teachers to recognize that fact and become more innovative. Some have found ways to play on student interest in slang to get them interested in learning seriously about language itself. One is Pamela Munro, professor of linguistics at UCLA. At the height of the Valley girl craze in 1989, she got her students to publish a dictionary of slang that has been republished every four years since then.

Among terms in the latest (2009) edition, *U.C.L.A. Slang 6*, were *schwa*, a synonym for *wow*, as an example of pulling new words out of thin air; verbal blends such as *eargasm*, the sensation of beautiful sound; *bromance*, love between two males; and shortened words such as *presh* for *precious*.

Another English professor who has become an expert on American slang is Connie Eble of the University of North Carolina. She says she specializes in "using the slang of my students to illustrate the forms and meanings of words and their histories." As S. I. Hayakawa said, "Slang is the poetry of everyday life."

Other lures to help language teachers reach out to today's youngsters include music, money matters, and Internet commentary. Some have also used social networks to teach how to write concisely. But where are all the studies of innovative techniques to help other teachers adapt to today's scene?

STREETS BECOME SCHOOLS

Is it any wonder why millions of youngsters learn their language arts in the streets, gyms, and playgrounds, especially in major cities, where the prevailing lingo is often set by African-American vernacular and Spanglish?

American black English was born when West African and Caribbean slaves hit the docks in England and its colonies in the seventeenth century. They added some welcome color and spice to the language that was still being formed by Shakespeare and God (through English translations of the Bible) as well as the public at large.

Since then, American black lingo not only has managed to retain much of its distinctive character but has played a leading role in the gradual transformation of formal English into today's informal language. The *dees*, *dems*, and *dose* of earlier centuries have morphed into a new vocabulary of words like *dis* for *harass*, *hood* for *neighborhood*, and *kicks* for *shoes*.

THE PC POLICE

At the same time, there has been a growing but largely hidden campaign to make educational materials politically correct. In keeping with the policy statements of teacher associations, such as NCTE and CCCC, many schoolbooks have been purged of any words deemed to be racist, sexist, elitist, or offensive to any other population group or perceived group.

Critics of such policies include Sandra Stotsky, professor of education reform at the University of Arkansas and former senior associate commissioner of education in Massachusetts. In her 1999 book, *Losing Our Language*, she declares that such political correctness is undermining children's ability to read, write, and reason.[12]

She cites a Scott Foresman reader for the fourth grade featuring an American family named Levin in which none of the members is related to any of the others. The two boys are Korean immigrants, each from different parents.

In 2003, Diane Ravitch, a former assistant secretary of education, focused further on this trend with a book entitled *Language Police: How Pressure Groups Restrict What Students Learn*.[13] Publicity for the book said, "If you're an *actress* or a *coed* just trying to do a *man-size* job, a *yes-man* who *turns a deaf ear* to some *sob sister*, an *heiress* aboard her *yacht* or a *bookworm* enjoying a *boy's night out* . . . [this book] has bad news for you: Erase those words from your vocabulary."

According to Ravitch, even Aesop's fable *The Fox and the Crow* was banned as sexist because a male fox flatters a female crow. Imagine if he had dissed her!

Ravitch's book reveals the persistent social pressure in the United States to avoid even a hint of prejudice toward certain groups of people. The goal is to satisfy everyone, but the result may satisfy only a few. A happy medium is elusive.

WHY A TEXTBOOK WRITER GAVE UP

Author Diane Ravitch quotes an anonymous textbook writer who broke under the strain:

> They sent 10 pages of single-spaced specifications. The hero was a Hispanic boy. There were black twins, one boy, one girl; an overweight Oriental boy; and an American girl. That leaves the Caucasian. Since we mustn't forget the physically handicapped, she was born with a congenital malformation and only had three fingers on one hand. One child had to have an Irish setter, and the setter was to be female. . . . They also had a senior citizen, and I had to show her jogging. I can't do it anymore.[13]

WHO NEEDS THE QUEEN'S ENGLISH?

Such pressures are especially resisted by creative writers. Novelist and poet Wolf Larsen wrote an essay titled "Who Needs the Queen's English?" in which he said, "Language must be the servant of the writer . . . [who] should throw off the straitjacket of grammar whenever necessary." He added, "Traditional grammar is not necessary in creative works. . . . Literature often has a rhythm that makes grammar unnecessary, just as a good verse has a natural flow that has made the rhyme obsolete."[14]

He also attacked the alleged discriminatory nature of Standard English. "Why should the mode of speaking of the most privileged members of our society be considered standard English? Why shouldn't the rich and constantly evolving language of poor blacks in the ghetto be considered 'standard English'?" He added that hip-hop lingo is "far more exciting and rich in contemporary culture than the 'standard' English of Park Avenue."

A SHOCKING AD

Even before the historic liberalization of grammar instruction by the NCTE in 1963, copy writers for advertising agencies were testing the bounds of acceptable grammar. The most noticeable breakthrough came in 1954 with an ad for R. J. Reynolds Tobacco Co. It said, "Winston tastes good like a cigarette should."

This slogan with the questionable grammar became one of the clearest public signals that a new type of English was emerging in the United States that no longer respected the outworn rules and standards of formal English inherited from the mother country.

Today, such an ad would not even be noticed for its language. But back then, pillars of culture went wobbly, English teachers were horrified, and millions of former students who had had problems in class finally got a whiff of emancipation. Until then, the language establishment had insisted that in such usage, *like* should be *as*, because of the conjunction function or something.

The Winston advertisement was so widely circulated on radio and television, including the *Beverly Hillbillies* and *The Flintstones*, that the otherwise undistinguished Winston brand soon rose to the top of the market. The poet Ogden Nash celebrated with a ditty saying, "Like goes Madison Avenue, like so goes the nation."

Many Americans finally felt like they could let all their linguistic frustrations hang out if such powerful commercial interests were so relaxed.

POWER TO THE PEOPLE

The ad also did what no previous event had been able to do: it essentially switched the power over language changes from the much-feared guardians of grammar to the general population, from professors, publishers, and lexicographers to street bums, pop musicians, and others on the lower and middle rungs of society.

Seven years later, defenders of the status quo were stunned further when Merriam-Webster published its *Third International Dictionary*, with no criticism of the word *like* for such usage. Strict constructionists, who were waiting for some support from on high, suddenly saw a major dictionary without a spine.

Language sticklers took another blow a few years later when ad writers gave the relaxed-grammar movement a new boost with a slogan for Tareyton cigarettes saying, "Us Tareyton smokers would rather fight than switch." Like the Winston breakthrough, this deliberate use of a grammatical "error" rocketed Tareyton up the sales rankings.

These new signs of Amglish were proving to be good for cigarette sales, not to mention lung cancer.

A SOCIAL REVOLUTION

Although it was not readily apparent at the time, the building language revolt became part of a broader political and social rebellion. The seeds had been sown by social rebels all the way back to the ancient Greeks and from them to Jesus, Buddha, St. Francis of Assisi, Luther, Thoreau, Gandhi, and Martin Luther King, to mention only a few who refused to conform to the norms of the day.

Signs of broad social change began a decade or so after the end of World War II. The most immediate prototypes were members of the Beat Generation, such as Allen Ginsberg, with their bohemian, beatnik styles of the 1950s. More sparks came in the next decade from yippies, hippies, and civil rights activists. Others were spurred by the assassinations of Robert F. Kennedy and Rev. Martin Luther King in 1968.

Many cities were hit by devastating riots. The city of Chicago added to the violence when the city's police force decided to crack down with a vengeance on political dissidents at the 1968 Democratic convention. Growing resistance to the draft and the Vietnam War added even more to the general dissidence.

The hippie movement emphasized a counterculture lifestyle including sloppy (or optional) clothes, pot smoking, and free thinking, mostly by young people. It was a natural convergence of beatniks, young rebels, college dropouts, draft resisters, environmentalists, and flower girls, in addition to poets, musicians, writers, and assorted dreamers. A popular bumper sticker was "If it feels good, do it."

At first the movement centered in the Haight-Ashbury section of San Francisco; then it spread to other cities around the country, including Greenwich Village, New York, where the *New York Times* is said to have fixed the letters *ie* to the word *hippie* instead of the letter *y* to avoid any reference to the hippy look.

The main themes soon went international, with colonies arising in Mexico, Chile, New Zealand, Australia, Britain, and Germany, among other places.

NEW MUSICAL THEMES

Music was the main vehicle of the movement, with lyrics almost always pointing toward a new informality of language and indifference to societal norms. This was particularly evident at the Monterey Pop Festival and Woodstock. Among the major stars were Bob Dylan and the Beatles, who helped spread the gospel of the psychedelic mindset in the BBC-banned album's closing song, "A Day in the Life," from their game-changing *Sgt. Pepper* album.

John Lennon struck a similar theme with his dreamy vocal, "I'd love to turn you on," a notion inspired by Timothy Leary's slogan, "Turn on, tune in, drop out." The Beatles did much the same with songs that stretched the limits of what a pop record could be, with shades of the Tibetan Book of the Dead, Lewis Carroll, and the folkie-turned-rocker Dylan.

Dylan took a different path to the same place, following folk and blues idioms to craft his own catalog of songs that referenced everyone from Shakespeare and T. S. Eliot to Bette Davis. His "Maggie's Farm" at the 1965 Newport Folk Festival was one of his final protest songs and was directed at the folk protest movement itself.

With their themes of protest, noncompliance, and love, these artists also were helping to shape a new American lingo, one that was free from the constraints and tensions of old-fashioned English.

CODIFYING THE PATTER

Out of all this came a 688-page *Hippie Dictionary* by John Bassett McCleary, a former hippie himself.[15] "Within recent history," he writes in the book, "no other counterculture has had as much effect on our lives and our vocabulary as has the hippie culture. . . . One must admit that the 1960s and '70s greatly influenced what exists today."

Adam Wojtanek, a blogger who calls himself "The Polish Hippie," goes further. He credits hippies and the Beatles not only for their broad cultural impact but for their powerful effect on American politics, resulting in ending the Vietnam War, granting amnesty to draft evaders, and helping to push gay rights, women's rights, and ecology out of the shadows.

Today's relaxed linguistic atmosphere was shaped to a great extent by hippie themes. Among popular words and phrases coined then and still in wide use are *hang in there*, *heavy*, *chill*, *cool*, *cop out*, and *head case*. The one word that seems to embody the whole story is *cool*, which not only survives but still flourishes today. A certain degree of cool seems to come from merely repeating the word as much as possible.

HERITAGE WORDS FROM HIPPIEDOM

It was really a *gas* to meet this *far out dude*. We *scarfed* down a pizza and beer, then *hung loose* until I got tired and *split the scene*. I came back to your *pad* so I could *crash* on your sofa. Do you *dig* it?

The world of computer nerds has also contributed new words to the nation's vocabulary, including *char* for *character*, *url* for a Web address, *prolly* for *probably*, *spam* for unwanted e-mail messages, and *asl* for age, sex, and location.

THE KEY ROLE OF BLACKS

No population group has contributed more to today's informal language than African-Americans. Whether in musical lyrics or street lingo, they have been at or near the cutting edge of almost all language changes since the early twentieth century. From early slave talk to spirituals, Dixieland, swing, rock and roll, rhythm and blues, and finally hip-hop, African-Americans have set the pace in pop music and pop talk to this day.

To a great degree, jazz and its lyrics sparked the trend. It all started in earnest in the 1930s and 1940s with the public's infatuation with the groovy jazz of Cab Calloway and Duke

Ellington. For many people, that love affair has continued right through to the present day.

Among the first words that joined the popular lexicon from the jazz world were *baby* for sweetheart, *balled up* for confused, *berries* for perfect, *big cheese* for the boss, *bimbo* for a tough guy or floozy, *dope* for hallucinogenic drugs, *john* for toilet, and *nookie* for sex.

THE WHITE NEGRO

Novelist Norman Mailer was one of the first to spot the vital links between blacks and whites that formed the basis of today's informal American English. It was in 1957 when he

spelled them out in the Fall issue of *Dissent* magazine in an article entitled "The White Negro."

In New York, New Orleans, San Francisco, Los Angeles, and Chicago, he wrote, white dissidents of the beat generation "came face-to-face with the Negro, and the hipster was a fact in American life. If marihuana was the wedding ring, the child was the language of Hip for its argot gave expression to abstract states of feeling which all could share, at least all who were Hip. . . . The hipster had absorbed the existentialist synapses of the Negro, and for practical purposes could be considered a white Negro."

Mailer himself was part of the white generations that grew up in the same early period and took to jazz and swing music so completely that they adopted much of the black lingual inflections as their own. He singled out the words *man, go, put down, make, beat, cool, swing, with it, crazy, dig, flip, creep, hip,* and *square*. "To swing with the rhythms of another is to enrich oneself," he added.

THE HIP-HOP CRAZE

Amglish has also been strongly influenced by the hip-hop movement with its rapid-fire lyrics set to the sound of heavy drums. The rapper style sprang from folk poets of the Caribbean and West Africa as well as Cuban reggae and good old American jazz.

Hip-hop was born in New York in the late 1970s and soon developed a powerful crossover appeal, eventually drawing many more white fans than black. It also spread its own culture to other venues, such as break dancing, veejaying, deejaying (like a video or disk jockey emceeing an event), and a wide range of mostly baggy clothing styles.

With the help of many eager corporate sponsors like Nike, Coca-Cola, and Sprite, hip-hop was soon spreading around the country and the world on the wings of Music Television (MTV) and Hollywood films such as *Wild Style*, *Breakin'*, and *Beat Street*. Its international appeal was largely due to its rebellious nature and language, which drew enthusiastic support especially from dissident groups in other countries.

To this day, it is considered smart and cool for whites to mimic black vernacular. Among the more popular hip-hop terms have been *boyz* for gang members, *chillin'* for acting cool, *hood* for neighborhood, and *my bad* for excuse me for fouling up.

Among the top artists have been Grandmaster Flash, Snoop Dogg, 50 Cent, Queen Latifah, P. Diddy, the Wu Tang Clan, and the great white hope, Eminem. Hey man, know wha'm sayin'?

HIP-HOP LIT

Although hip-hop has not generated much literature, at least one rapper claims his "gangsta" novels with sexually explicit language have sold well. He is Renay Jackson, one of the stars interviewed by Spencer Michels on the *Online NewsHour* in 2003. Jackson, who worked as a custodian for the Oakland (CA) Police Department, claims that one of his novels, *Oaktown Devil*, sold 35,000 copies.[16]

In response to a question from Michels, Jackson said, "In this neighborhood, just like the majority of neighborhoods I describe in my books, you have, like, killings, you know, drug dealings—look at that—you know, just like the everyday life of, like, you know, the urban streets." He says his audience is mostly young black males.

Michels also interviewed the publisher, Richard Grossinger, founder of North Atlantic Books in Berkeley, CA. "When I got the books," said Grossinger, "I thought that they were actually pretty wonderful. They were good stories, they were funny, they had great dialogue in them, and they had a quality of authenticity that you just couldn't fake. I would say it would be disappointing to sell less than 50,000 of each of the books. And they could well sell up in the hundreds of thousands."

INNOVATIVE LANGUAGE

Of all the continuing chroniclers of the American language, PBS has been the leader among major media with its running segment, *Do You Speak American?* It was in 2005 when rap star JT the Bigga Figga said on the show that black language

is constructed of—alright let me take it all the way back to the slave days and use something that's physical. All the slave masters gave our people straight chitlins and greens, you feel me, stuff that they wasn't eating. But we made it into a delicacy. Same thing with language . . . .

They didn't want the slaves playing drums because we was talkin' through the drums . . . you feel me? So through the music, that's kinda like going on now with the rap thang. It's ghetto music. People talkin' about they issues and crime and, you feel me?

Along the way, hip-hop terms have gone both national and international. *Bling-bling* even found its way into the linguist's bible, the *Oxford English Dictionary*.

FREAKED-OUT VALLEY GIRLS

By the 1980s, the language-generating process shifted briefly to mostly white high school girls in California's San Fernando Valley who added their own versions of the new lingo with their giggly *barf me out*, *fer sure*, *as if*, and *totally*, as in "she totally freaks me out." Subsequent massive usage of the word *totally* has effectively reduced its wattage close to zero.

Perhaps their greatest single contribution to today's lingo, however, is the word *like*. Nobody at the time could have predicted how prevalent this four-letter word would become in the following decades. It was already stretched thin as a noun, verb, adjective, and conjunction. To all these duties, Valspeakers used the word to introduce a quotation, such as, "I was like, 'What are you doing, girl?'"

A FAMILY WORD GAME

Making up words has become a private joy for many American families. One of the first to notice the tendency was Allen Walker Read who called it "the effervescing of language" in a 1962 article for *American Speech*, the American Dialect Society's magazine. More recent is a 2007 book by Paul Dickson, *Family Words*.[17] He lists such gems as *mudwaffles* (chunks of mud brought into the house on running shoes), *lurkin* (a single sock whose mate is lurkin' around somewhere), *granny hangers* (loose flaps of skin hanging from an old person's upper arm), *rump spring* (an old stuffed chair with a spring showing through), and *garpe* (one family's name for grape jelly because of a misspelling on a shopping list).

These high-pitched contributions to the language were, like, immortalized in the 1983 movie *Valley Girl*, which by now seems "so yesterday," a further bit of Valspeak. Just as Valspeak was dying out in 1995, another movie, *Clueless*, revived

it briefly with a printed guide to the movie's slang. The film added the ubiquitous *whatever* and helped to consolidate the ever-present *like* and *you know* in the nation's vocabulary.

Seeking to capitalize on the informal language trend, Steve Jobs, the clued-in chief of Apple, launched his famed *Think Different* ad slogan in 1997. His willingness to risk offending savvy tech buyers with this questionable grammar proved to be a smash hit. By this time, few could have been offended by the ploy pioneered earlier by Winston cigarettes.

COSBY'S COMPLAINT

After 2000, hip-hop sales dropped significantly while many critics cited a deterioration in the lyrics and an increase in

raunchiness and misogyny. An even bigger decline in sales in 2005 might have been sparked by professional funny guy Bill Cosby. The wildly popular African-American TV star, who has a master's degree in education, blew his top in a 2004 speech at Howard University at a ceremony honoring the Supreme Court decision on school desegregation.

"Just forget about telling your child to go to the Peace Corps," he said. "It's standing on the corner. It can't speak English. It doesn't want to speak English. I can't even talk the way these people talk. 'Why you ain't?' 'Where you is?' . . . I blamed the kid until I heard the mother talk. Then I heard the father."

He said it wasn't like this when he was growing up black—and kind of bilingual: "You used to talk a certain way on the corner, and you got into the house and switched to English. Everybody knows it's important to speak English except these knuckleheads. You can't land a plane with 'Why you ain't?' You can't be a doctor with that kind of crap coming out of your mouth."

Cosby was politely applauded at the predominantly black university, but some African-American leaders objected later, pointing to the contribution of black dialect to world culture and citing the popular art of Langston Hughes, Ray Charles, and others. In response, Cosby pointed out that such artists all spoke what he called standard American English.

THE FILTER PRINCIPLE

The drop in hip-hop sales should not have been surprising to close observers with a broad view of history. The key might be called the natural filter principle of language. When pollutants like oil threaten the life-giving qualities of ocean water, a natural cleansing action seeks to bring the pollutants under control. Likewise, when a language becomes too polluted, natural cleansing action takes over.

The U.S. Supreme Court essentially backs the same principle. It has left the matter of obscenity up to the general public by ruling that the key factor in determining whether something is obscene and therefore prohibited is whether it violates "contemporary community standards."[18]

It is possible that Cosby's speech helped slow the flow of language that threatened to destroy its own habitat. It is also possible that radio jock Don Imus's excesses caused a similar effect. On April 4, 2007, the foul-mouthed faux cowboy flamed out when he called the Rutgers women's biracial basketball team "nappy-headed hos," a term for African-American whores. He didn't object when his producer sitting with him added another racial insult.

After getting some immediate flack, Imus issued a quick apology. But some people called for his dismissal because of his long record of making similar remarks. A week later, NBC, citing many complaints, canceled its simulcast of the show, *Imus in the Morning*. The next day, CBS canceled the radio version, citing its sudden concern about the effect of such language on young people, "particularly young women of color."

These reactions followed many public protests, essentially votes of individuals, some of whom had sought publicity for

a book or for themselves on the show. There was yet another turn of the giant filter, perhaps the key one. It was the decision of seven sponsors to pull their ads, including American Express, General Motors, Staples, Sprint, GlaxoSmithKline, Nextel, and Procter and Gamble. There's nothing like a pulled ad to get a talk jock's attention.

So, in effect, it was the general public's decision, the filter principle, that an important line had been crossed, and the violator needed to be ostracized. It was like the natural way that Amglish depends on the broad public, not the language police or broadcast censors, to set the ground rules in the final analysis.

Such a process does not work well in formal English with all its bewhiskered rules and self-appointed guardians of the sacred relics that range in age from four hundred to over two thousand years old. Look at how ineffective parents, teachers, and politicians have been in stamping out obscenities through censorship and punishment over the long haul.

HIP-HOP REVERBERATIONS

Only a few weeks later, it became apparent that the Imus case was reverberating in the hip-hip world. A campaign by the late C. Delores Tucker in 1995 to tone down some of the *bitches*, *hos*, n-words, and porno stuff was finally coming to a head. Punctuating this campaign was a further drop in album sales. Her widower said the Imus case had "brought about a revival of the struggle she waged" against lyrics demeaning to women.[19]

The drop in sales was also enough to cause Russell Simmons, the multimillionaire owner of the hip-hop label Def Jam and fashion house Phat Farm, to call for a voluntary ban on bad words and the imposition of guidelines. His decision coincided with an NAACP attempt to kill racist and sexist terms.

Simmons told a reporter that he was responding to "public outrage" that could lead to a "nasty discussion" and possible censorship.[20] He added that decisions in the music business tend to be driven more by commerce than ethics, and sales of unedited albums regularly have exceeded those of edited ones. Of course, public sales are simply votes in the marketplace.

The natural language filter is always working, but it doesn't always bring dramatic results. Howard Stern is living proof of it. The man whom the *New York Times* once called "the King of All Four-Letter Words" effectively conquered earthly talk radio in 2004 and moved to outer space as a talk host for Sirius XM for an obscene amount of money, said to be $500 million over five years.

The difference between Stern and Imus may be a matter of humor and precision. The precision of the former can help blunt his excesses; knowing exactly where to draw that line can neutralize the filter. Imus apparently had to learn how to limit his remarks. Stern already knew. In general, people enjoy a certain amount of smutty talk, but it has to be judicially tempered in the long run.

THE WASH CYCLE IS ON

There is evidence that all obscenities and vulgarisms are going through a cleansing initiated by the general public, without any dramatic threats, movie codes, or too much bleeping. People who speak Amglish don't normally distinguish between vulgarity that is acceptable and vulgarity that is not. They tend to let the general public draw the line.

Take the age-old *S-O-B* put-down, for example. Excessive usage over many years appears to have weakened the phrase to the point where it is now used more as a term of endearment between two men, as in, "How's it going, you old sunovabitch?"

Another word that has lost its shock value is *suck*. Originally used to describe a basic human action, from nursing an infant to a sex act offensive to some, it is almost exclusively used now to express simple displeasure or disgust without implying any off-color inference.

The actual date of death for *suck* as a vulgar term was August 2, 2006. That was the day when the establishment media endorsed its new viability. The online magazine *Slate*, a branch of the *Washington Post*, declared the word "completely divorced from any past reference it may have made to a certain sex act." Since then, it has acquired enough—should we say dignity?—to be used in formal documents, such as memorial notices honoring the dead.

An example of such use is the following passage in a woman's paid memorial notice on a newspaper obituary page of the *Post* that same year to tell her long-deceased mother, "Life down here sucks." (The name and date are omitted to avoid identifying the person involved.)

Since then, the phrase has become quite common, especially for that very special message sent to honor a dead relative online or in a newspaper obituary page, or in remembrance of a birthday or anniversary.

A Google survey revealed more than five hundred such phrases, nearly all of which were in a funereal context. When the word *stinks* was substituted as slightly less offensive than *sucks* for grieving people, only three examples showed up. *Sucks* is clearly preferred over *stinks* for such somber occasions.

ACLU SOLVES *ASSHOLE* PROBLEM

When the American Civil Liberties Union heard that Pennsylvania state police had issued more than seven hundred citations to people for mouthing off at such things as an overflowing toilet, it sued them. The suit included Lona Scarpa who faced a $300 fine for calling a motorcyclist an asshole for swerving toward her.

The case was settled in January 2011. The police paid Scarpa $17,500 and agreed to stop arresting people for such things. A year earlier the city of Pittsburgh paid $50,000 to a man who had been cited for making an obscene hand gesture.[21]

THE FADING F-WORD

Even the f-word, which used to be the best attention getter, seems to be fading. To describe a sunset with it, for example, is apparently no longer considered hilarious. And when Vice President Dick Cheney publicly told Senator Patrick Leahy of Vermont to "go f— yourself," hardly anybody was surprised or shocked. The word apparently has lost some of its shock value through massive overuse.

Much of the credit for the new atmosphere should go to the many comedians who have played a big role in this self-cleansing action. Few have been more ingenious than Jon Stewart of *The Daily Show* on Comedy Central. By uttering the f-word so often while knowing it will be bleeped, he spares the millions outside the studio audience from hearing the word and, of course, laughing at his jokes. That's a sacrifice beyond the call.

ARE *LIKE* AND *YOU KNOW* EXPLETIVES?

It turns out that expletives may not necessarily be dirty words after all.

The 1972 edition of Webster's *New World Dictionary* lists two meanings of *expletive*: an oath or filler in a sentence. Webster's *Third New International*, which was published in 1961, lists two meanings: the first is *filler*, the second is *obscenity*.

So if a verbal filler is an expletive, would words like *like* and *you know* be expletives, obscenities, or just plain fillers?

However, don't call the f-word dead yet by any means. In early March 2011, three songs with that word in their titles or choruses made it to the Top 10 Hits, one helluva bleeping development. It was part of an effort of the music industry to get away from the restrictions of censored broadcast media now that the Internet and related devices have become such a viable alternative. It also might have meant that the giant word filter was temporarily too clogged to work efficiently.

Meanwhile, raw obscenities seem to have lost favor with some politicians. They now seem to prefer more original terms. This is another linguistic area where George W. Bush set the pace early. When he came to publicly label his longtime adviser Karl Rove, for example, he did not choose a worn-out term like *sh—head* or *a—hole*, which might have been more apt for Rove. Instead, Bush chose to call him "turd blossom," a Texan expression from the pasture. Only a genuine language leader could be so original and effective.

Neither government nor self-appointed language censors have the right stuff for reducing the smut quotient in movie and media fare. The only workable process is the Amglish filter that lets the public make its own decisions in the natural course of things. The trouble is that it sometimes takes too f—ing long.

Another area where such standards are still in flux, however, is the blogosphere, especially where space is provided on websites for individuals to post personal comments. The amount of vitriol and filth on some websites appears to be reaching saturation levels. But it apparently has not yet hit the level for the filter of public judgment to change the pattern.

COMEDIANS DO THEIR BIT

Comedy is central to language development because it requires an atmosphere for experimenting with words, an openness so essential to the healthy growth of language.

American comedians have been especially blessed in having such a quirky language to work with. For example, everyone knows there is no English in English muffins, and there's no ham in a hamburger or egg in an eggplant. And if the plural of *mouse* is *mice*, then why isn't the plural of *house hice*? Only a speaker of English would know that stars are visible only when they are out and that lights are not visible when they are out.

These and the many other quirks of the language weren't purposely put there; they were inherited from people even more idiosyncratic than Americans, the English. They spent centuries developing such peculiarities before shipping them across the sea for Americans to add their own touches.

Mark Twain was quick to see the humor in the design. And he took full advantage of it. A champion wordsmith, he tried to reduce the length of words and simplify spelling without success. Tina Fey, the latest winner of the Mark Twain award, also likes to play with words. One of her favorites is *snart*, a combined sneeze and fart.

Among those who helped exploit the sometimes charming defects of English during the key Amglish-forming period of the 1970s to 1990s were comics Roseanne Barr, George Carlin, Bill Cosby, Redd Foxx, Dick Gregory, Jay Leno, David Lettermen, and Richard Pryor.

A HOMEMADE CONBOBBERATION

Many early Americans busied themselves making up words to fit their rough, frontier lifestyle. Among the beauties were *ringtailed roarer* (hearty guy), *ramsquaddle* (to beat up), *conbobberation* (ruckus), *hornswoggle* (cheat), *screamer* (beefy man), and *rambunctious* (unruly). So the *ringtailed roarer* no longer creates a *conbobberation* when he *hornswoggles* the *rambunctious screamer*.

Or in today's terms, will the *digerati greenwash* their *Blu-Rays* via *cloud computing* and get enough *street cred* to *virtualize* their *carbon footprint*? I'm jus sayin.

THE SEVEN BAD WORDS

Carlin in particular was a master of originality with words. His magnum opus, *Seven Words You Can Never Say on Television*, made it all the way up to the Supreme Court in 1978 in a case involving the government's right to regulate so-called indecent and obscene material on the public airwaves.[22] The Supremes didn't get any of the jokes and ruled in favor of censorship by the Federal Communications Commission.

The ruling effectively banned the seven words—ones that every adult knows—from programs likely to be seen or heard by children. In reality, however, the ruling boosted Carlin's fame and inspired even greater usage of the contested words both in and outside broadcasting. There's nothing like prohibition to make a banned item wanted even more.

Contemporary comedians continue to have a ball with their native language, particularly with their ability to get laughs with neologisms. Recent additions to the list include Stephen Colbert's *truthiness* and the recycled *frenemies* and Jon Stewart's labels for things like *Mess-O-Potamia* and *Californigaytion*.

GROUNDBREAKING AUTHORS

The first major author to go native—and graphic—was Harriet Beecher Stowe, who used the language of slaves and their masters to take a strong stand against the way most blacks were treated in the United States. Her gutsy book, *Uncle Tom's Cabin*, published in 1851, sold more copies than any other in the nineteenth century.

Samples included "Never was born," persisted Topsy. . . . "Never had no father, nor mother, nor nothin'. I was raised by a speculator, with lots of others." Other quotations from characters in the book reflected her strong sentiments: "Treat 'em like dogs, and you'll have dogs' works and dogs' actions. Treat 'em like men, and you'll have men's works."

The passionate novel brought her fame but also much grief, mostly from the Southern establishment and its sympathizers in the North. Many people blamed her—or credited her—for instigating the Civil War that resulted in freeing the slaves. She was also accused of oversympathizing with blacks by imitating their language and describing their woes so graphically.

Strong reactions continued long after her death. As the era of political correctness set in, there were numerous efforts to denigrate her book for not representing slave life more accurately. In 1949, author James Baldwin blamed her for not fully revealing "the inherent evils of a bad system." Talk about late-hitting a little old lady when she's down—and under!

Stowe's realistic style became the pattern for T. S. Arthur's *Ten Nights in a Bar-Room*, published three years later. Like Stowe's book, this was a clever use of common speech to plead for a cause, in this case temperance. These books helped break the template of stuffy British literature and plot a more permissive course for American literature.

AN ACTIVIST LEXICOGRAPHER

Even some dictionary makers can be called pioneers when they aim both to codify the language and change it. Noah Webster was a rare bird who fitted both job descriptions. He led a move not only to Americanize the language brought across the ocean but to inventory the vocabulary that existed mostly in the latter half of the eighteenth century.

His *Dictionary of the English Language* in 1806 was the first major U.S. dictionary. He also performed surgery on many British words by removing the final *k* in words like *musick*, dispensing with the letter *u* in words like *colour*, and transposing the last two letters in words like *centre* and *theatre*. But he failed to kill silent letters such as the *b* at the end of *thumb*, for which he got the third finger from some critics.

Webster's activism was largely inspired by Samuel Johnson and the famous dictionary he published in 1755. Johnson was of two minds as well. He vowed to "fix" English by excluding new and bawdy words while publishing off-color ditties such as this one by one Sir John Suckling: "Love is the fart of every heart; it pains a man when 'tis kept close; and others doth offend when 'tis let loose."

CONTRIBUTING AUTHORS

The previously mentioned Mark Twain was another brush cutter for early Amglish with his lovable creations, Tom Sawyer and Huckleberry Finn, and his efforts to use the vernacular of black and white boys playing together in the South of the early 1800s. His *Adventures of Huckleberry Finn*, published in 1876, starts out, "You don't know me, without you have read a book by the name of *The Adventures of Tom Sawyer*, but that ain't no matter." H. L. Mencken called Twain "the first American author of world rank to write genuinely colloquial and native American."[23]

Mencken also singled out author Walt Whitman for his "romantic confidence" in the role of "iconoclastic and often uncouth American speechways" in fostering U.S. democracy. He said Whitman's "central purpose [was] to make war upon the old American subservience to 18th century English pedantry and open the way for the development of a healthy and vigorous autochthonous language in the United States." Whitman's love of slang led to a pioneering magazine article entitled "Slang in America."[24]

Mencken's words for Whitman could also describe himself. His mammoth book, *The American Language*, is a tour de force of the American language's history. Other trailblazing pioneers of language in the twentieth century include Ring Lardner and his depictions of street and bar talk in New York; Studs Terkel, with his quotes from unsung heroes; Norman Mailer, with his bold-at-the-time obscenities; and Tom Wolfe's gripping descriptions of affluent society's seamier side.

The lowercase poet e. e. cummings deserves special mention for his playful spelling and syntax. He caused a stir in the early twentieth century by occasionally signing his name in lowercase letters and deliberately mixing up words, both of which devices were due later to spread into common usage. Among his verbal inventions that didn't catch on were *mud-luscious*, *puddle-wonderful*, and *eddieandbill*.

JUMPING FOR JUNIE

Then there's the more recent Junie B. Jones, the controversial character in a series of books from Random House originally aimed at the kindergarten crowd but later upgraded to older ages and expanded into movies, games, and coloring pages. With her informal language, Junie indirectly promotes Amglish—and book sales—with clever misspellings and questionable grammar in phrases like "I hearded that name" and "runned away."

In other words, she fits into the Amglish world, much to the dismay of many parents who wonder how their offspring can ever learn formal English by reading such material. Other parents swear that their children have been inspired to do more writing and reading than they otherwise would have. They add that the use of the vernacular by Barbara Park, the creator of Junie B., is similar to Mark Twain's classic use of it in *The Adventures of Huckleberry Finn*, one of the top American classics.

Which set of parents is closer to the truth?

If the question is whether Junie has harmed the ability of young Americans to communicate, the answer seems to be no. One glance at the degree of texting, phoning, and e-mailing by youngsters shows that they have no problem making themselves understood by their peers while greatly enjoying the process.

If Huck caused no serious problems for readers of his day, Junie B. is not likely to do so today.

CLEANING UP HUCK

As the year 2011 began, however, Twain's book became the center of another type of controversy stemming from his use of the word *nigger* 219 times in the book. The racial issue came up like thunder when it became public that Alan Gribben, a language professor at Auburn University in Alabama, had decided that each word should be replaced by the word *slave* in a new edition, even though the slave in the book had been freed.

Gribben explained that the n-word had become so explosive at a time of growing political correctness that the book might become one that people praise but don't read. "It's such a shame," he told the Associated Press, "that one word should be a barrier between a marvelous reading experience and a lot of readers."[25]

The news story set off a national debate over whether the much-read literary classic should be changed after so many years. Most critics said Twain himself would have objected. He once wrote, "The difference between the almost-right word and the right word . . . is the difference between the lightning bug and the lightning."

But Comedy Central's Stephen Colbert supported the idea of whitewashing American history and suggested that the job had only begun. "It's great to have the n-word out of Huckleberry Finn. Now get to work on the Moby D-word."

Except for his joking response, it looked like another example of the language filter starting to work, this time not on common obscenities but on the use of overtly racial terms. As this is written, not all the votes are in, but the Amglish system of allowing the public to make the ultimate decision on controversial language seems to be working, though often slowly and erratically.

This chapter has described some of the pioneers who helped create the informal language that is replacing formal English in the United States. The next chapter will describe how the new American lingo has spread around the world.

The New World Lingo

GO OUT MUBARAK

—Words on a man's forehead in Tahrir Square, Cairo,
February 8, 2011

This crudely crayoned message in Cairo's Tahrir Square is only one of many examples of the informal English penetrating the rest of the world. Such signs are part of a growing strategy by people in other countries to solicit international support for their causes by getting news microphones and cameras to pick up their crudely framed English words and convey them to the centers of world power.

Also illustrative of the U.S. influence in the Arab uprisings in 2011 was the central role played by American-based social networks such as Facebook, YouTube, and Twitter. The spark that lit the populist fires in Egypt was a graphic photo on Facebook of the distorted face of an Egyptian man beaten to death by police. When it became public on February 8 that the man who posted the photo online was Wael Ghonim, the Middle

81

East manager of Google, the news brought out the largest crowd in Egyptian history to honor him.

These words and photos on the Internet were additional proof, if any were needed, of the worldwide influence of American language and pop culture. According to the Voice of America, there were 5 million users of Facebook in Egypt when the public demonstrations began there on January 25.

Five years earlier, Amglish had already penetrated the very birthplace of English so thoroughly that the nation's soccer superstar David Beckham blurted out the following words about his children: "The homework is so hard these days. It's totally done differently to what I was teached . . . and you know, I was like, 'Oh my God, I can't do this.'"[1] The new lingo had obviously gotten in too deep for him or anyone else to kick the habit.

Normally, Brits don't like to play second fiddle to their former colonies, but when it comes to keeping current with the latest patter from across the pond, they are obviously turning out to be little more than lapdogs in bulldog drag.

BLAME THE YANKS

For centuries, American slang has invaded the rest of the world with its jaunty words and phrases, with the likes of *hang loose*, *hit the sack*, and *chill out*. For just as long, the British have been annoyed at the reverse invasion, particularly the slippage of grammar, just one of the things they blame on Americans and their bloody television, music, and movies. It's not just Beckham's "I was like" but his casual grammar that annoys the English upper class, yet seems to set just the right tone with his teammates, fans, and chroniclers.

In fact, so-called Modern English has been broken since its birth four centuries ago. Shakespeare recognized it in *Henry V* when he had the king plead with the young French princess to accept his advances with the words: "Breake [disclose] thy mind to me in broken English."[2] A few years later, Thomas Heywood, in *Apology for Actors*, called "our English tongue . . . the most harsh, uneven and broken language of the world."

More recently, the fracturing seems to have become an asset. By 1984, the bits and pieces were well on their way to becoming the world's premier language when Hendrik Kasimir, a Dutch physicist, wrote,

> There exists today a universal language that is spoken and understood almost everywhere: it is broken English . . . the much more general language that is used by the waiters in Hawaii, prostitutes in Paris and ambassadors in Washington, businessmen from Buenos Aires, scientists at international meetings and by dirty-postcard-picture peddlers in Greece.[3]

Amglish was partially certified in 1997 when the Linguistic Society of America formally declared it "incorrect and demeaning." The Society is one of many such groups that just don't get what's happening. There can be no doubt any longer that informal American English has become the lingua franca of the world. The more fractured it becomes, the more popular it seems to get.

THE POWER FACTOR

When it came to spreading English around, of course, the Brits got a big head start. The key to the early expansion of language outside its birthplace was raw power, the strength to subjugate nations and dominate their trade. This was the path the language took to Australia, New Zealand, India, Kenya, and other British colonies, most of which later became independent.

India is an example of how English can be forced upon a non-English-speaking nation via military muscle. It was exercised through the Asian nation's legal system, business community, school system, and government agencies. No one knows how many Indians are fluent in English today. But Aharon Daniel, a native of India and world-renowned blogger on the subject, says, "After Hindi, it is the most commonly spoken language in India and probably the most read and written."[4]

The United States has also used muscle to spread its brand of English, particularly in Puerto Rico and the Philippines. More recently, the Pentagon has established nearly eight hundred military bases around the world and taken on the mantle of the world's policeman. But unlike the British in India and the Japanese, who forced their language on Korea and Malaysia during World War II, the Americans have not forcibly imposed their language on other nations.

The USA brand has flowed more from becoming the world's first superpower in World War II. The war saw millions of GIs spread their four-letter words along with their Luckies, Camels, Cokes, Pepsis, Budweisers, Jeeps, Levis, and Spam to all who survived the rain of American bullets and bombs.

AMERICAN OUTREACH

Behind all these brands was America's basic ability to supply enough equipment and supplies to outproduce the Germans and Japanese and to dominate the world's economy ever since.

Among the major initiatives adding to the powerful appeal and spread of English, especially American English, were

- the huge Lend-Lease program in which the United States, before declaring war, supplied shiploads of food and other essential supplies to many countries opposing the Germans;
- the American occupation of Japan and major parts of Germany, including Berlin, after the war;
- the Marshall Plan, which provided more than $100 billion in current dollars to Allied nations after the war for reconstruction; and
- the Cold War, a series of initiatives led by the United States to put pressure on the Soviet Union from the end of World War II to the fall of the Berlin Wall in 1989.

The linguistic effects of all this indirect diplomacy on people already in the English-speaking world were felt as far away as Australia. According to Sidney J. Baker, the author of a book on Australian slang, "It was not until the war sent half a million American troops across the Pacific to Australia that Australians began to realize how little they knew about American slang."[5]

THE CULTURAL INVADERS

As military hostilities ended, a still more massive invasion brought American pop culture, such as movies, music, radio, and TV shows, as well as consumer products of all types. Hollywood films, which had already gained many fans overseas with actors like Mickey Mouse, Clark Gable, Myrna Loy, and the Marx Brothers, took over the world's screens in a serious way. And they have reigned ever since, even though India's Bollywood produces more films.

Among the more popular American ambassadors in this period were Ford, Chevrolet, Frigidaire, Maytag, and of course Glenn Miller, Fats Waller, and Benny Goodman with their jazz and swing. Although the lyrics were often superficial and nonsensical, they had enough pizzazz to be swallowed with great relish by foreign admirers.

Other major players included international media giants based in the United States. They saw big opportunities early and took maximum advantage of them. Among the leaders were Disney, Time Warner, and News Corp. All joined the race for dollars, leaving few people untouched by American language and culture. Lane Crothers, a professor at Illinois State University, explains how these firms came to spread so much pop culture to such a receptive world:

> The early transnational corporations that produced movies, music and television programs took advantage of permissive laws, an open culture, a diverse audience and ideal filmmaking weather to build global empires of audiovisual entertainment.[6]

This gave American producers an advantage in competing for the mass international entertainment audience that exists today.

BUILDING MARKETING MOJO

The cultural invaders consolidated their beachheads by building promotional bridges in the form of marketing tie-ins, such as Mickey Mouse ears and *Star Wars* T-shirts, almost all accompanied by the American lingo. Other leaders were the industrial giants General Motors and General Electric, as well as the inviting images of Ronald McDonald, Colonel Sanders, Papa John, Starbucks, and other popular franchisers.

Over the years, American business firms have also contributed the power of employment by establishing branches, setting up phone banks abroad, and hiring workers far from U.S. shores to staff these operations, especially today in India, Latin America, and the Philippines, where wages tend to be low. The government has no recent numbers for outsourced jobs, but Forrester Research Inc. of Cambridge, Massachusetts, estimated in 2010 that 3.3 million service jobs will have moved offshore by 2015.

TOO MUCH ENGLISH ABROAD?

Over many years of visiting foreign countries, my wife and I have often been frustrated by an unseen yet ever present language barrier: the nearly unanimous tendency of residents of those countries to respond in English to our questions in their own languages.

We always want to practice our foreign languages but find it difficult to do so because of this barrier. We attribute foreigners' determination to their desire to (1) practice their own English, and (2) show how multilingual they are. Many fellow travelers have confirmed the same problem.

Most people in other countries can readily recognize foreign accents and learning errors as they spar with us—and win—over language practice time. Dammit.

Wrapped up in all these diplomatic—and profitable—bundles has been the popular lingo of the United States with its imaginative words and phrases, including *hip, kooky, oddball*, and more recently *nerd* and *homie*. Young people have led the way, with their consistent urge to appear awesomely *cool* by voicing just the right American words and phrases before their peers.

DOMINANT GENES

American English has increasingly dominated almost everything in the international spectrum, including communications, science, research, business, sports, navigation, technology, travel, and journalism.

Another big factor in spreading the language has been the British and American governments in their roles as presenters of news—as well as indirect propaganda—to the rest of the world. As the war ended, the British Council was created presumably to promote English around the world. Or was it to offset the spread of American English? That's what Paul Z. Jambor, a teacher of English as a foreign language, says was the main reason. He calls it an example of English language imperialism.[7]

Other examples of what might be called indirect language imperialism have been the American institutions known as Radio Free Europe (RFE), Radio Liberty (RL), and Voice of America (VOA). By selecting and editing news items and choosing interviewees, the United States cannot avoid the propaganda charge, but at least it is not the crude, overt kind. RFE/RL, which started in 1950, claims to reach twenty-one countries in twenty-eight languages. VOA, which was born in 1942, claims a daily audience of 125 million.

Since 1959, VOA has also offered a free course called Special English, which strips the formal language down to 1,500 words. By clicking on various icons on the VOA website, people can learn how to order coffee at three language skill levels, while instructors of English as a second language (ESL) can get free workbooks and other teaching aids.

LANGUAGE CONVEYORS

Nothing can spread English like English itself. Today's international flood of English words essentially began with the electric telegraph invented by Paul Julius Reuter, a German, in the mid-1800s and the first transatlantic radio transmission by Italy's Guglielmo Marconi in 1901. Reuter built a news service, later headquartered in London, that scored its first scoop with news of Abraham Lincoln's assassination in 1863.

British and American entrepreneurs eventually turned these foreign inventions into the international communications monster that we all recognize today. The British Broadcasting Corporation (BBC), today's largest broadcaster, began in 1922. American broadcasters soon jumped into the business, but none has come close to the international reach of the BBC as a disseminator of news.

Telecasting the news is even more American English–oriented. CNN, based in Atlanta, was the first news network to broadcast worldwide by satellite, followed by BBC and Sky News, a News Corp operation. Other worldwide networks with English newscasts include France 24; Al Jazeera (Arabic), Deutsche Welle (German), TRT (Turkish), RT (Russian), and TV Globo (Portuguese).

British and American companies have also dominated the print form. Their combined efforts have resulted in blanketing the world with news and commentary. Today's big news organs include the London dailies, the British *Economist* weekly magazine, the *Wall Street Journal* and the *International Herald Tribune*, which is owned by the *New York Times* and printed in Paris. The *Journal*, the most widely circulated newspaper in the United States with more than 2 million daily buyers, also has Asian and European editions.

AD WORDS THAT WENT AWRY

The Leo Network, an international ad agency, collects language mistakes that big companies make when they advertise worldwide. The boo-boos include:

- A Braniff airline ad suggesting "Fly in leather [seats]," only to discover later that the word in Spanish for leather meant "Fly naked."
- Clairol advertising a curling iron called "Mist Stick," only to find out that the first word is slang in German for manure. Yet "Mist Stick" has an unmistakable sound.
- Coca-Cola advertising in China with the word *Ke-Kou-Ke-La*, then discovering that the word means "bite the wax tadpole" or a "female horse stuffed with wax."
- Chevy's Nova, a GM car, whose name in Spanish means "Won't go."

The *International Herald Tribune* has affiliations with newspapers in many other countries, including Kuwait, Japan, South Korea, Israel, Russia, Greece, Spain, Egypt, India, and Pakistan. The typical arrangement is for the local paper to circulate an English edition of its own paper with the *IHT*. Its circulation is relatively small—200,000—but its influence on world affairs is considerable.

Books also have become conveyors of the language. Millions of people around the world have become fans of British and American authors such as Nathaniel Hawthorne, Mark Twain, George Orwell, Aldous Huxley, T. S. Eliot, John Grisham, William Faulkner, Ernest Hemingway, Tom Wolfe, and Norman Mailer. For individual results, however, none can compare with J. K. Rowling and her series of *Harry Potter* books, with more than 400 million copies in circulation.

INTERNATIONAL BIZ ENGLISH

Especially since the turn of the twenty-first century, English has been not only preferred but required for doing almost any business internationally. Sales presentations, conferences, and negotiations are now conducted almost entirely in some form of English, whether formal or informal.

For business, it is also obligatory to train employees, manage websites, do research, prepare advertising materials, and be able to converse with customers all over the world in English, if not also in their native language.

At Tieto, a Finnish company with international business, its English-language website offers the services of its 17,000 "experts" in solving information technology (IT) problems for business primarily in English. An attorney for the firm Feodor Bratenkov says, "It would be just impossible to conduct any international business without having such a common means of communication as English."[8]

In fact, many firms conduct their own classes in English and even use it in interoffice memos. Almost every industry or large group also has its own special words and phrases that constitute a unique dialect. Examples are Insurance English, Automotive English, Oil Industry English, Legal English, and even Illegal English, a term used to keep students from speaking English at Middlebury Language Schools in Vermont.

Inevitable in all corporate English, of course, is a shadow lingo, a type of corporate slang that author Lois Beckwith calls "corporate bullshit." Her 2006 book of that name says, "More people than ever before are using more bullshit."[9] The volume is filled with such terms as *bring to the table*, *crackberry* (addiction to a Blackberry phone), *deets* (details), *feedback*, *focus group*, *glass ceiling*, *micromanage*, and *move forward*.

CORPORATE JARGON IS ALWAYS SHOVEL READY

Here is my sampling mostly from Beckwith's book: When setting up a *PowerPoint presentation*, it is *mission critical* to *circle the wagons* before making a *world-class commitment*. Every participant will need some *face time* with a real *people person* and a chance to *kick the tires* of the plan to be *networked*. First, a *heads-up* about going for the *low-hanging fruit* and not considering the *mission critical*, which should be an excellent *teachable moment*. If you don't see a *paradigm shift* by *the end of the day*, you might be considered *roadkill*.

ENGLISH IN WORLD ADS

Similar terms are used to sell American goods and services abroad. In fact, American English is the most used language for advertising virtually anything across international borders, whether the advertiser is based in the United States or elsewhere.

Ads are usually tailored differently from country to country, not so much because of different languages but because of different customs and circumstances. They also must comply with the various laws and regulations dealing with decency and how much nudity can be shown in advertisements.

It pays to have an intimate knowledge of the local scene. The McDonald's restaurant chain found that out through experience. In 1996, an adult comic magazine named *Viz* filed suit, charging that some ad words had been stolen from the magazine's TopTips column. McDonald's settled the issue with cash in lieu of Big Macs.

Non-American companies also advertise frequently in English when seeking business from other countries. As a result, many of the magazines produced and sold in other countries, such as Italy's *Panorama*, are flush with advertisements for American products or services with product names and descriptive text in English.

For example, *Panorama*'s February 25, 2010, issue carried ads saying "Brother at your side," "James Bond Deluxe Collection," the "business magazine" economy; "Fusion = Fusion" for Infiniti cars; "McCain: It's All Good" packaged food; "Spring/Summer Collection" for a fashion item; "Elegance goes sporty" for the Audi A6; plus "THIS IS IT," the headline over the lead story on Michael Jackson's revival from the dead.

HUMOROUS USES OF ENGLISH ADS

The Internet is full of ad images with imaginative uses of English that can cause a chuckle from expert users of the language. Bona fide samples from the Internet include: TOILET WOMAN—SLIP CAREFULLY; WELCOM TURIST—WE SPIK INGLISH; BE AWARE OF INVISIBILITY; CAUTION—BUTT HEAD AGAINST THE WALL; NO PARKING ABOVE THIS SIGN; PLEASE DO NOT EMPTY YOUR DOG HERE; PLEASE DON'T MAKE CONFUSED NOISE WHEN CHANTING; DO NOT GOSSIP—LET HIM DRIVE; FOOT WEARING PROHIBITED; TOILET—STAY IN YOUR CAR.

Ads in English seem to have a special cachet. In Holland, a study by Jos Hornikx of Radboud University in Nijmegen showed that ads in simple English were preferred even over similar ads in Dutch and held their own when more complicated language was used.[10]

The advantages of using English for international advertising are numerous. One is the positive image created for the product or service; another is the chance that potential customers will use the ad to learn more English or sharpen what they already know. One study showed that students who frequently watch subtitled TV and movies do better on translation tests. Not surprisingly, playing computer games in English also helps.

MUSICAL MISSIONARIES

As already stated, American popular music has played a huge role in propelling informal English to the larger world. The phenomenon goes all the way back to the early days of jazz in the United States. The New Orleans trumpeters, saxophonists, and singers of the 1920s and 1930s had no idea that they were doubling as missionaries of slangy English to the world as well as the nation.

From jazz to bebop, from blues to rhythm and blues, from rock and roll to country and western, from soul to hip-hop, music has played a big role in spreading the language through lyrics. Behind the star-studded artists have been the corporate sponsors, broadcasters, record companies, and of course Hollywood in promoting the words and music.

A huge new wave of American influence through music began in the 1960s as teenagers in other countries began latching on to songs and lyrics with a frenzy. They rocked and rolled, did the twist, and collected singles and LPs of such stars as Joan Baez, Neil Diamond, Jimi Hendrix, the Grateful Dead, and Simon and Garfunkel.

So popular were such performers that their music became integral parts of "American studies" in high schools across Europe, according to Monique Briendwalker, who grew up in France during that period. She says Paul Anka was a musical guest at every party of teenagers in her area of Brittany.

Through the 1970s and 1980s, it became cool for European young people to go American not only in song but in clothing styles, and in the slang they spoke to each other. Casual became the way to dress, with basic jeans, tee-shirts and sneakers, a style that swept the world and remains dominant to this day.

Briendwalker lived these trends, later booking concerts for Columbia Records stars all over Europe. She says almost every teen learned enough American English to sound adequately cool and smart to their peers. She adds that the language became so universal that it was often difficult to link the youngsters to their native countries.[11]

THE KEY ROLE OF MTV

Viacom's Music Television (MTV) started in 1981 with a 24-7 music video format that soon became an international art form. The channel later branched into many sister channels as well as different types of programs. Since then, it has built a world audience that exceeds 50 million online followers.

In a 1999 interview, MTV's David Flack was asked to describe what part English had played in music sent to Southeast Asian youths. Flack, the senior creative director for Asia, said,

> It's in music where the English language is the biggest success. A lot of bands, even local bands, sing in English: It's the language of rock and roll. One band in India recently argued they could sing in their local language and were quite successful, but generally Indian bands sing in English. . . . [But] as soon as the band wants an international audience . . . it has to be in English.[12]

MTV has also delved into various international causes such as the struggle for social justice as it has sought to build its appeal to young people around the world. Some observers, however, say that such moves were motivated by earlier criticism that MTV was too much in the pocket of the record companies to take a sincere stand on anything.

As an example of its power to set patterns, MTV created the popular acronym *VJ*, the video version of a disk jockey. The music channel also grabbed some fame, wanted or not, as the producer of the 2001 Super Bowl halftime show in which Janet Jackson's bared breast outperformed the football teams.

More recently, the organization has developed a network of TV channels aimed at devotees in more than fifty countries in their local languages.

THE POWER TO ATTRACT

Perhaps the biggest reason that so many young people abroad have latched on to the latest words and music from the United States has been to show their peers that they are right up to the minute with the latest trends. Ever since the war, as Briendwalker says, it has been considered smart to insert American slang into conversations with their peers. It is just as chic to chomp into a Big Mac with fries in Paris or to grab a foot-long at a Subway in Bahrain or St. Petersburg.

The unspoken but clear message conveyed by these widely known meeting places at almost every busy intersection in the world has been, it's time to learn informal American English the easy way: while enjoying the latest Hollywood movie or TV soap or franchise meal with a large Coke or Pepsi to go, and of course with an American song on an iPod.

ENGLISH OBSCENITIES ARE SEXY ABROAD

Jeremy Wallach reports that young Indonesians use English obscenities for romantic purposes because they are safer and sexier than their
own languages. The terms, which they get from broadcast music,
apparently free them from inhibitions they otherwise would feel.[13]

In South Korea, young musicians use English to construct an image
of menace or sexual daring as well as to emphasize the contentious,
uninhibited nature of their art.[14]

Jannis Androutsopoulos, a linguistics professor at the University of Hamburg, explains, "*Cool, wicked, chill, dope, nerd.* Young people around the world use this kind of slang to show they're connected to American pop culture." She says such language "is powerfully expressive because—paradoxically—it is both exclusive and global" since it is not available at school or in the mainstream media.[15]

Androutsopoulos added that the Amglish term *flipped out* becomes *ausgeflippt* in German, *flippato* in Italian, *flippe* in

French, and *fliparismenos* in Greek, while English partially translated into German results in *abchecken* (check out), *ausflippen* (flip out), *abhangen* (hang out), and *abrippen* (rip off).

Even more significant is how English in all its forms has penetrated the world far from its traditional stomping grounds in Europe and its native lands. What does the language have that has made it so welcome so fast?

Braj Kachru, an emeritus professor of linguistics at the University of Illinois recognized some basic reasons at a relatively early stage. Drawing on ten studies in 1986, including ones in India, Israel, Singapore, and Sri Lanka, he concluded that the key was its power to connect diverse people to the outside world. In his book, *The Alchemy of English*, Kachru writes, "English initiates one into the cast that has power and, more important, that controls vital knowledge about the miracles of science and technology."[16]

As for the preference for American English, he refers to the fact that "America has become a phenomenon of envy and emulation . . . for it combines technology, scientific progress and, above all, power."[17] Kachru does not go into the inherent qualities of English itself, but others have pointed to its basic characteristics that somehow allow a high degree of adaptability, flexibility, and assimilation that are not as prevalent in other major languages.

THE TESL INDUSTRY

With all these factors pushing English into every nook and crevice of the globe, it is not surprising to see a great expansion of the business of teaching English as a second language (TESL). Although almost all governments have made English compulsory in school, the effort has fallen far short of public demand.

Many public school courses have been slow to keep up with changing language styles and often wind up being more perfunctory than thorough. So parents become willing to pay almost anything to arrange lessons for their children, because they know how important the language can be for personal success in today's world.

Many adults also have reasons to either brush up on their knowledge of English or learn it from scratch. They know that even rudimentary English can help them get a job with an international business firm. And they know that such knowledge can make them appear more worldly wise—or should that be word wise?—in the eyes of their peers.

As a result, teaching English outside public school has become the fastest-growing branch of the business. Although there are some large firms with many branches, most of the instruction is done by small firms or individual teachers attuned to local conditions.

The first requirement for anyone seeking instruction is to learn the basic acronyms determining whether lessons are for English as a second language (ESL) or English as a foreign language (EFL). Teaching jobs are either TESL or TEFL. Of course, EIL means English as an international language.

The distinction between ESL and EFL is important because standards for using English as a second language are usually far lower than those for acquiring fluency in a foreign language through a formal course. The difference has become a subject of debate among instructors, with some demanding the establishment of standards for EIL.

The issue was addressed seriously in 2009 by Ahmet Acar and Paul Robertson in an article for a professional language journal. Not surprisingly, they concluded that since today's international English "is no longer viewed as a homogeneous language but as a heterogeneous language with multiple norms and diverse grammars," setting standards doesn't make sense.[18]

Most of the language teaching abroad produces Amglish, not formal English. That's apparently all that many nonnative users want or need.

AMGLISH AS A BRIDGE

Amglish has also become a linguistic bridge for communicating between countries where it is not already the native tongue. In 2005, when France's premier Jacques Chirac met for the first time with Angela Merkel, the German premier, they reportedly conversed in Euro-English. The term refers to Standard English mixed with translating and learning errors by non-English speakers.

Another version of the bridge concept is the way young Scandinavians have come to use Amglish when communicating with Danish, Norwegian, and Swedish friends. Older

---

A FOUR-LETTER WORD FOR ALL

The word is STOP, the term for cautionary highway signs worldwide.

In almost every country, the familiar white-on-red sign warns motorists to come to a halt before proceeding farther because of a busy intersection or highway. The word got its international debut as a sentence ender in telegrams.

Stop signs were already widely used before 1978 when the Vienna Convention on Road Signs and Signals, the international body for bringing uniformity to travelers, voted to approve such use.

THE AMGLISH BRIDGE

generations were able to understand other Scandinavian languages without using bridge language. But English was not as prevalent then as now.

The bridge metaphor also works in China, according to Ji Shaobin, professor at Wenzhou College of Profession and Technology. "English," he says, "is not [only] the language for us to speak with Americans, the British or any other native speakers. Rather, it is the common language for us to communicate with Japanese, Koreans, Thais, Singaporans and other Asians and people from developing countries."[19]

In India, the bridge syndrome is more domestic in nature. English serves as a sort of lingua franca among Indians who speak different languages.

Informal English also serves as a middle ground on international athletic fields. In 2006, World Cup Soccer required all of its referees to have a working knowledge of English because it was the language known best by players and coaches. Four years later, the refs were required to add a knowledge of obscenities in English in order for them to know when and whether to penalize a certain player. Or was it so some refs could add a little verbal abuse of their own?

English can also be a middle ground within mixed population groups, such as fellow employees in a business firm. David Rohde, a former writer for the *Christian Science Monitor*, described one such group in an Australian factory. It included Cambodian, Samoan, Maltese, Greek, and Latvian workers all complaining about their boss in the lingo they each knew to some extent. Rohde added that in Thailand, Russians, Pakistanis, Japanese, and Germans make phone calls to each other by shouting out numbers in English or "something like it."[20]

EUROPE'S SECOND LANGUAGE

But the European Union doesn't want to buy a language bridge. Its policy has been to encourage many tongues over any one. It says every member nation should teach at least two languages in school, though it doesn't say which languages they should be.

Despite the EU's stand, private efforts have been made to devise a Europeanized Standard English in order to provide a common lingo that is easy to learn, uniform for diplomatic and trading purposes, and able to save substantially on translation costs. One of the areas of possible improvement cited is the fifteen different English spellings of the *sh* sound, namely the words: *shoe, sugar, issue, mansion, mission, nation, suspicion, ocean, conscious, chaperon, schist, fuchsia, pshaw, fashion,* and *crucifixion*.

According to Juliane House of London's *Guardian Weekly*, the main reason the EU has not made English the official second language is that "the French with their traditionally superior position in Europe cannot accept the decline of their own linguistic power."[21] By 2001, 47 percent of EU residents already spoke English well enough to hold a conversation, according to a Eurobarometer survey.

The reason nobody has devised a simplified form of English that works for everybody is that it has to be naturally formed in the streets, in the suites, in the workplace. Planning can't help the language process.

WORLD CONFERENCE LINGO

Meanwhile, organizations dealing with global issues have quietly but surely made English the preferred lingua franca for conferences. Participants must acknowledge its role as a bridge language not only for general sessions but for informal task forces. They confirm it each day with their mouths and mouses.

Such use of English for international meetings and conferences started in earnest with the United Nations, where English is the working language for all conferences and publications. For example, at the United Nations Convention on Biological Diversity that represented 190 nations and drew 15,000 participants to Tokyo in October 2010, all the proceedings were in English.

John Fitzgerald, a lawyer for the U.S.-based Society for Conservation Biology, says that not only were all discussions in English but delegates who expected to have any effect on the proceedings had to have more than a casual knowledge of the language in order to handle the sophisticated questions that would arise. The usual pattern for such international conferences, he added, is to translate plenary sessions simultaneously into major languages but to use only English in subcommittees and task forces where the basic work gets done.

Other international conferences in 2010 that operated primarily in English included the Conference on the Future of Science that met in Venice and the World Conference on Computer Science that met in Cancun, Mexico. No longer does the language of the host city qualify if it is not English. There are more than 10,000 international organizations.

The December 2010 ceremony in Oslo awarding the Nobel Peace Prize to Liu Xiaobo, the political dissident held in a

Chinese prison, was also conducted in English. Nothing new for Scandinavians.

UNIVERSITY ENGLISH

Another indication of how extensively English has spread, especially among young adults, is the number of English courses offered in overseas universities. According to Diane Spencer of University World News, the number tripled from 2003 to 2008. She said the Academic Cooperation Association in Brussels found approximately 2,400 courses, almost all at the master's level. Most of the courses were in countries north of the Alps. In keeping with the cosmopolitan nature of the times, more than two-thirds of the students were from another country.

A more dramatic example of the growth of English in European universities occurred in March 2009 in Groningen, Holland. Marlies Hagers reported in the now-defunct *nrchandelsblad* that hundreds of students met in the Academieplein Square in that city as university Rector Frans Zwarts lifted a glass of champagne on the steps of the university building and toasted in English: "To a very successful next academic year. I wish you all the best." Earlier that day, he had given a speech in English at the official convocation.

A proposal to make English the official language of instruction at Dutch universities was made first in 1990 by education minister Jo Ritzen as a necessary step to attract more international students. At the University of Amsterdam, 105 of 170 master's programs were already given in English. As expected, however, Ritzen's plan ran into some opposition from establishment types, who bemoaned the dilution of their national character.

BAD ENGLISH WORKS GOOD

For American travelers, it is now routine to encounter both formal and informal American words and phrases almost everywhere. Typical was the experience of a group of American psychiatrists, including John Kafka of Bethesda, Maryland, who were invited to teach medical students in Odessa in 2007. When a visitor asked a group of students what language they normally spoke, they replied almost in unison: "Bad English." Call it what you will, "bad English," "broken English," or Amglish, it is sweeping across the world, and most people are being just as good humored about it.

At the same time, English's chief rival and predecessor in the lingua franca business has steadily been losing stature. In 2009, the European Commission reported that the percentage of its documents drafted in French had decreased from 40 percent in 1997 to only 11 percent. In response, Michel Serres, a French author, quipped, "There are more English words on the walls of Paris than German words under the Occupation."

GREEK AND LATIN ROOTS

Europeans should welcome English as a family member. Their ancestors contributed greatly to its formation over the centuries. Today's English is an amalgam of almost every earlier language of the Western world going back to Greek and Latin and the Indo-European languages that preceded them. Many of these early roots have bubbled up the language chain to attain their present forms in dictionaries.

Latin words include *animal, animosity, audacious, bonus, calculus, conjugal, diary, disciple, domain, effort, feminine, final, fortune, judge, lunar, marine, matron, maximum, pedestrian, pessimist, rural, suburb,* and *village.*

Greek words in English include the following, starting only with the letter *a*: *abyss, academy, acme, acoustic, aerobic, agnostic, agonize, allegory, anchor, anemia, angel, angina, angle, apathy, arial,* and *athlete.*

When I asked John Robertson, who runs the wordinfo.info website featuring Latin–Greek cross-references, if he had ever compiled a list of English words with Latin or Greek roots in a specific dictionary, he replied, "So many new words are being created in our modern times from those two sources that no one can keep up with the new entries."

THE FRENCH CONNECTION

Outside of the basic Greek-Latin inheritance, French has had the next biggest influence on English. That is mostly because of the Norman invasion of England in 1066 and the subsequent control of that nation's governing powers for nearly three centuries. As many as 30 percent of today's English words are of French origin.

Some common examples in English are *ballet, blasé, brunette, bureau, café, chauffeur, cliché, communiqué, critique, en route, entrée, gaffe, liaison, omelet, sabotage, silhouette,* and *unique.*

During the period under French control in England, country folk tended to speak a mixture of French and English called Anglo-Norman, while city folk spoke mostly French. The turning point was the devastating Black Death in 1348–1350. It tended to kill off more city folks than country ones, thus making the latter, who spoke rudimentary English, especially influential in lifting English into the dominant role.

Since then, French authorities seem to have been burning because of their failure to win the language war in Britain. Led by the forty *immortels*, the French Academy has been fighting—and losing—a guerilla war of tongues much of the time since Cardinal Richelieu established it in 1635.

The standard-setting group requires all companies operating in France to communicate with employees in French. It also bans certain non-French words from being used by the media and other elements of society. It even sets the percentage of broadcast music that must be in French. The latest requirement is 40 percent.

One of the fiercest fighters for the fading glory of *la langue français* has been Helene Carrere d'Encausse, the first female permanent secretary of the academy. In 2002, she delivered a formal speech vigorously defending French and decrying the many "anglicisms that make proper French words die." She noted sadly that the best French is now spoken in Warsaw, Tel Aviv, Dakar, and other distant *iles de France*. She ended by saying that French is taught in 118 countries, all of which consider it a "superior language."

Former premier Jacques Chirac agrees. In 2006, a "deeply shocked" Chirac stormed out of an EU summit in protest when a French businessman addressed the delegates in English. This was the same Chirac who had reportedly used diplomatic English in dealing with Germany's Merkel. Also in 2006, an unnamed French subsidary of an American company was fined $800,000 for providing computer software to its employees in English only.

French President Nicolas Sarkozy has also been defensive, complaining of "snobism" by French diplomats who prefer English.[22] The defensiveness is based on the popular phrase: "*Mon pays c'est ma langue*" (My country is my language). As

Monique Briendwalker, a French teacher in the United States, puts it, "It's a fight to survive as a culture, as a power, as a nation."[23]

SIGNS OF CHANGE

But there never has been any doubt as to which side was winning. It has always been the brash linguistic invaders. One of the signs of change came in 1990 when the National Textbook Company in Lincolnwood, Illinois, published its *Dictionary of Faux Amis* by C. W. E. Kirk-Greene. Starting with its Frenglish title, it indirectly documented the way English was altering the French language by including a large number of English words used by the French. Examples are *book*, *building*, *cake*, *car*, *cherry*, *chips*, *crash*, and *legs*.

---

500 FALSE FRIENDS IN FRENCH

The *Dictionary of Faux Amis* contains approximately five hundred "false friends," mostly French words that have a different meaning in English from what even a speaker of French might expect, plus words with several meanings to choose from. For example, *aimer* can mean "to love" in French while its false friend is "to aim." Likewise, the word *appel* can mean both an appeal and a telephone call.

The author also points out that *c'est un as* is not the insult it sounds like but just the opposite: "he or it is top class." Another example is *monnaie*, which normally means money or currency. But to say you don't have any *monnaie* in French may mean you're loaded but don't have any change.

Never mind the trends. Full speed ahead, say French authorities. As recently as March 2008, the Academy issued sixty-five pages of prohibited words, including *blog*, *e-mail*, *fast food*, *podcasting*, *supermodel*, and even such terms as *shadowboxing* and *detachable motor caravan*. Among the directives to the French people were: use *acces sans fil a l'internet* for Wi-Fi, *diffusion pour baladeur* for iPod, *toile d'araignee mondiale* for the World Wide Web, and *courriel* for e-mail.[24] *Bonne chance* with all that.

FRENCH ED CHIEF GIVES UP

Less than six months later, however, at least one key French official quietly hoisted the white flag of surrender. Xavier

Darcos, the French education minister, admitted that the key to success was not better French but better English. He was quoted by the London *Daily Mail Online* as saying that using poor English had suddenly become a "handicap" because international business was being conducted in that language. He added more money for teaching English to students who did not have money for private lessons.

A year later, French author Eric Semmour sadly noted that the French elite had also given up fighting English. "They don't care anymore," he told a reporter. "They all speak English, and the working class . . . don't care about preserving the integrity of the language either."[25]

According to a 2004 poll by the Pew Research Center, 68 percent of those aged sixty-five and older in France agreed that young people need to learn English to succeed in the world today. Pew found similar results in other European countries.

RETURNING TO GERMANY

The old language is flooding back. That's what many Germans must be thinking as English words inundate their nation and the world at a time when most Germans know enough English and American words and expressions to converse with each other in English. The first signs of what we now call English came largely from West German, Frisian, and Nordic invaders of the British Isles midway through the first millennium.

Since then, the German and English languages have shared many of the same words as well as grammatical structure. There are no reliable figures to show which European nation has become the most Americanized linguistically, but all signs point to Germany.

Jurgen Flach, a native German who became a U.S. citizen while serving as general manager for an international pharmaceutical company in the States, says most Germans learn English in high school as a second language in a nation where 90 percent of the music is in English.[26] Now retired in Germany, Flach adds that there are many areas in large German cities where only English is spoken.

Dorothea Baerthlein, writing for TOPICS *Online Magazine*, says that in Germany she does *aerobics classes*, *warms up*, *cools down*, *goes jogging* and *shopping* for a *T-shirt*, *sweater*, and *shorts*—using all those English words before going to a *meeting*. It's all part of a long sharing process.

Among German words imported earlier into English are *frankfurter*, *hamburger*, *kaput*, *kindergarten*, *rucksack*, *schaden-freude*, *wanderlust*, and *zeitgeist*.

IS THERE A LIMIT?

However, there is a growing backlash against using English and Denglish, the linguistic marriage of Deutsch and English. Some Germans feel that the constant injection of English into their society is threatening the existence of German itself.

One leader of the resistance is conservative politician Erika Steinbach, who has said, "Without English or the parody of it that is Denglish, it no longer is possible to get by in daily life in Germany. Millions of Germans are at a loss . . . because so many products and ads are presented to them in a foreign language."[27] Steinbach and others have tried to enact laws restricting ads in foreign languages.

There have also been complaints about the dominance of English in science and research, where Germans have always been internationally prominent. Other subjects allegedly under siege include economics, mathematics, natural sciences, and technology.

The German Language Association has also been trying to stop the proliferation of Denglish. A sauerkraut named Walter Kraemer, the organization's director, calls the German use of English "pseudo-cosmopolitan exhibitionism." Yet he accepts words like *sex appeal* that have become part of the German language. What riles him most are words for which there are perfectly good German substitutes.[28]

ALL LANGUAGE IN THE MIXER

English is not the only language in the Cuisinart. French and Japanese have merged in part into what is called "Franponais." It is essentially the misuse of French words in Japan. Other terms for it are "Flanponais" and "Flançais," with optional pronunciations.

The mixture comes from the fact that many Japanese think it is stylish to spout French terms in the fields of fashion, cuisine, and hairstyles. But few Japanese can actually speak French fluently.

As a result of such complaints, the country's railroad, Deutsche Bahn, was forced to remove signs in English from station areas and to replace them with signs in German. So a sign saying *Kiss-and-Ride* turned into *Kurzzeitparkzone*, and a sign for *Hotline* was changed to *Service Nummer*. These changes have not stopped the company from selling *tickets*, giving out *service points*, and boasting of a washroom known as *McClean*.

Lufthansa, the German airline, took the hint several years ago when it switched from its slogan "There's No Better Way to Fly" to a German equivalent. And the German Transport Minister announced at the end of 2010 a list of 150 English words and terms that were *verboten*. Claiming to have the support of Chancellor Angela Merkel, Peter Ramsauer said the move was taken to preserve the German language from words like *babysitten*, *rebooten*, and *downloaden*.

AUSSIES GET A GUTFUL

Europe is not the only place in linguistic turmoil. By 2003, Premier Peter Beattie of Australia said he had had "a gutful" of Americanisms and was not going to take it anymore. "America might control the world," he said, "but we must control and keep our language. . . . We don't need *diapers*, *candy*, *ketchup*, *trash cans*, and *fries*—we've got *nappies*, *lollies*, *rubbish tins*, and *chips*."[29] He added that his island nation doesn't want to be the fifty-first state.

Objections to the American influx apparently went much deeper. According to Sidney J. Baker, the previously cited Sydney linguist, "Australians have suffered a lingual melancholia that has left them uneasy about their future. . . . They have been told so often by the misinformed that their own slang lacks originality and has been imported in bulk from America that they have lost confidence in themselves." Baker quoted author I. L. Bird as saying in her *Australia Fix* in 1877 that there was a tendency even then for Aussies "to adopt words which are rather American than English in their use."[30]

EFFECTS ON OTHER LANGUAGES

It is only natural that the revolution in English, with its growing prominence in the world, would cause changes in other languages. This is even true for Asian languages that use ancient images as letters and symbols, a system that presents the greatest contrast to the Roman letters of English.

In Japan, the presence of English is huge, and it is having a profound effect on the Japanese, according to Alexander Michaelson, an American student living in Japan. He notes a distinct movement away from kanji, the characters inherited from the Chinese, toward more and more katakana, the phonetic system that represents foreign words in Japanese.

In China, English is cutting deep into the learning of Chinese by those who were born there. Zhang Ming-jian, an associate professor at Qingdao University, reports that "too much focus on English has led to a lack of enthusiasm in learning the Chinese language and culture and decreasing proficiency in the mother tongue as well."[31]

In South Korea, English has replaced Chinese as the source of most loan words since World War II, when the nation was freed of Japanese rule. Since the Korean War, the American influence has increased greatly. Joseph J. Lee, a graduate student at San Francisco State University and a former teacher in Korea, says English words picked up phonetically include *coffee*, *orchestra*, *cherry tomato*, and *plastic bag*, the Korean equivalent of *vinyl envelope*.

In Greece, where the natives are especially friendly to American tourists because they spend so much more money than others, everybody connected to the travel business knows

English. That includes ferryboat crews, hotel clerks, taxi drivers, police, shopkeepers, and guards at historic sites. In fact, English is creeping into almost every corner of Greek life and raising concerns about the ability of the language to keep its famed heritage as the oldest European language.

Many Greeks have become fed up with the incursion of English words. In 2001, a group of intellectuals including professors and playwrights launched a verbal war against Greeklish, claiming that there was an "unholy plot" by international computers against demotic (modern) Greek. Words singled out for derision included *erkodission* for *air conditioning*, *frikaro* for *freak out*, *komputeraki* for *laptop*, and *rockatzis* for a fan of rock music. Ten years later, it was clear that the purists were losing the fight.

OBAMA, JAPANESE ENGLISH TEACHER

President Obama was in office only a short time before he unknowingly became a linguistic as well as an inspirational symbol with a worldwide following.

His inaugural speech was circulated internationally on CDs and in books. In Japan, for example, 200,000 CDs and more than half a million books containing the speech were sold within nine months, according to the *New York Times*.

It reported that most Japanese bought it because the speech used simple English terms that can help the Japanese learn English. Others reportedly bought it for the inspiration they got from it.

THE KILLER INSTINCT

English seems to have an ability to fracture or kill other languages and turn the results into new mixtures with their own special vocabularies. According to Paul Z. Jambor, "the Maori language in New Zealand was slowly displaced by English in most domains until its recent comeback." He added that several aboriginal and North Amerindian languages "were in a sense killed by the English language."[32]

Meanwhile, English is rapidly turning Spanish into Spanglish, particularly in the United States. Since the fifteenth- and sixteenth-century Spanish explorers, such as Cortez, de Leon, and Pizarro, there has been a constant movement of Spanish speakers into the northern hemisphere and what eventually became the United States.

The flood of migrants since then has apparently crested recently because of the economic slowdown and stricter policing of the Mexican border. But by 2009, the U.S. Census Bureau reported that there were about 45 million Hispanics who speak Spanish as their first or second language and that more than half of these people speak English well.

But many Latino immigrants don't learn English and may get along fine for a generation with their native Spanish, since many public notices are now in both languages. Second-generation Latinos invariably learn English in school and become proficient in Spanglish, both of which which can serve as stepping stones to better jobs and lives.

Lin-Manuel Miranda's play, *In the Heights*, dramatizes this process with real-life Latinos singing and verbalizing, like, "Foo, you know! Spanish mixed con Ingles mixed with Spanglish y tambien the occasional local/urban dicho?" as the program notes say.[33]

THE SPANISH ACADEMY

Spain has its own language control group, the Royal Spanish Academy, but it is much less aggressive than its French

equivalent. In 2009, the academy issued a new grammar book for the nearly half a billion people in twenty-two countries that have Spanish as their primary language.

Among the English words officially accepted by the Spanish Academy were *esponsor* (sponsor), *cederrom* (CD-ROM), and *striptease*. Other words undergoing an extended process of acceptance are *market*, *parking*, and *mitin* (for meeting). The academy also issues dictionaries that give the official spelling of Spanish words, which are supposed to set the pattern for all Spanish speakers.

In 2010, the group decided to drop the two letters *ch* plus numerous accents and frills from the Spanish alphabet. That action caused a stir in South America, where President Hugo Chavez of Venezuela claimed that he would henceforth have to be known as "Avez," even though his name would not change.

In Mexico, the daily *El Universal* scoffed at the elimination of the letters and said the action should not be accepted by the Spanish-speaking nation. The paper was most upset by the procedure of having its national language manipulated by "a conference room abroad."

But the academy claims it has been trying to keep up with natural language changes, not trying to stop them. Another factor may be in play. According to Ilan Stavans, the author of *Spanglish: The Making of a New American Language*, Spain still harbors a grudge against Anglo-Saxon culture stemming from the defeat of its Spanish Armada in 1588. He says that may explain why there is so much disdain in Madrid for any incursion of English words into the Spanish language.

Meanwhile, Spanglish is becoming so entrenched that it is being institutionalized in the form of books, music, and permanent vocabularies worldwide.

In an interview with the *Barcelona Review*, Stavans said that until the previous decade, Spanglish was known as "lowly regarded *jergo callejero* [street jargon]," but now it has graduated to a "decisive cultural phenomenon" that is rapidly being standardized by radio, magazines, and business firms, and it's even featured on a line of Hallmark cards.[34]

COUNTRYWIDE BANS

Numerous nations, in addition to France and Spain, have sought to curb imported words. In 1999, Brazil imposed a ban on the use of any foreign language on public documents. But the action has not stopped the spread of American English throughout the country.

In 2006, Iranian president Mahmoud Ahmadinejad apparently had received one too many e-mails. He issued a ban not only on that word but some two thousand other foreign words that were being used in his country. As a result, Iranians could no longer order pizza by mobile phone or chat on one with forbidden words. Pizzas became *elastic loaves*, cell phones became *companion phones*, and a chat grew into *a short talk*, all in Farsi.

It wasn't until December 2010 that China's Communist government began to dig out from the English onslaught. It ordered Chinese publishers and website owners to say *bai bai* to all foreign words, particularly English ones, as well as the concoctions of Chinglish. Radio and TV outlets were already working under such restrictions. The government said the flood of foreign words had "seriously damaged" the purity of the Chinese language and had caused "adverse social impacts" on the cultural environment.[35]

However, some people familiar with the situation in China feel that English already has too many roots to be pulled up by force. Roscoe Jean-Castle Mathieu of Shenzhen, China, told BBC that "almost everyone has a self-chosen English name, and they refer to each other with English names, such as Billy Cheng and Vivian Wong." "JR" of Nanjing added that he still hears lots of English acronyms such as *OL* for "office lady" and *DINK* for "double income, no kids."

SIDEWALK SOPHIE

Anna Sophie Lowenberg, a young American resident of Beijing, made a video showing herself asking random Chinese on the sidewalks of that city if they had an English or American name. Almost everyone she asked said yes. Names included "Samanfar" (for Samantha), "Tony," and "Smacker," an odd one for a young woman. Lowenberg spotted a young male store employee wearing a name tag that said "Susan." He laughingly told her that his boss had put it on him.[36]

A complete ban would hit one city especially hard. This is Yanshuo, a hiking and rock-climbing hub in southern China, with English-learning schools on nearly every block. Eleanor Terry, a New York teacher, reported in 2009 that the city was teeming with international college students "running around with teams of Chinese schoolchildren in matching neon colored t-shirts asking tourists, 'Do you have time to help us? What's your name? What is your favorite food? and Do you like China?" She said the Chinese children were spending the summer—like a summer camp—learning English.[37]

She added that the city was very Western friendly, with a restaurant/bar "that plays only country music and serves a dozen different types of hamburgers"—with side orders of Chinglish.

CRAZY ENGLISH: SHOUT IT OUT

You've heard of Shouting Methodists. Now there are shouting Chinese. They yell in English in order to learn it. The idea was conceived—and patented—by Li Yang who scored well on an important English test in college by practicing it at top volume.

Believing that anyone can learn another language by shouting it out, he started his teaching method in 1994. He also wants everyone to know that he has more than 20 million practitioners. Let's hear it.

OTHER RESISTANCE

In 2008, an influential Italian cultural organization, the Dante Alighieri Society, called for elimination of anglicized words in Italy like *il weekend* and *lo stress*, which it called *Anglitaliano* and others call *Italglish*. An informal poll by the society cited other English words that Italians have used for years, such as *shopping* and *bookshop*. The society's plea was drowned out by more Americanisms.

In Slovakia, using an English sentence or two on the air in 2010 could lead to a severe penalty, according to *The Slovak Spectator*. Andy Hillard, a British musician living in Bratislava, found that out when he appeared on a Slovak TV show.[38] When Hillard appeared not to understand a question, host Stefan Hrib switched to English, and Hillard answered in English. The brief Q&A was not translated or dubbed.

Three years earlier, Slovakia's Council for Broadcasting and Retransmission had lifted the BBC's radio license to broadcast in Slovakia because its content was in English, a violation of Slovak law.

ALL THINGS WIKI

Amglish is akin to the wiki world, because the two concepts share the same type of freedom, simplicity, and international power. Ward Cunningham, who sired the wiki family, chose to name it after a "Wiki Wiki" airport shuttle in Honolulu where the word means *fast*.

The progenies include Wikipedia and Wiktionary, both free and editable by others who have expertise to offer. They have been criticized for errors and for allowing readers to edit the data. But the error rate has been reported to be nearly the same as for traditional encyclopedias. And the editing process has been tightened. Like Amglish, everything wiki is a work in progress.

FAMILY DIVISIONS

The worldwide popularity of English can also present big problems down the road for individuals and families who don't speak it but face pressure to have their youngsters learn it in school. Parental motives may be innocent enough—to help their children succeed in today's English-dominated world—but the result may be children who cannot or will not speak the native language of their own parents and grandparents.

AS ENGLISH SPREADS, INDONESIANS FEAR FOR THEIR LAN-GUAGE. That was the headline over a *New York Times* article by Normitsu Onishi who quoted several mothers of schoolchildren facing that dilemma. "They know they're Indonesian," one mother of three was quoted as saying. "They love Indonesia. They just can't speak Bahasa Indonesia. It's tragic."[39]

Onishi wrote that a person's language essentially determines his or her social status, and that until the end of the Suharto regime in 1998, Javanese was at the bottom, Bahasa Indonesia was above, Dutch was the tops, and English was discouraged. Since then, he wrote, English has become the new Dutch.

Aimee Dawis, a communications teacher at Universitas Indonesia, told Onishi, "Now the dilution of Bahasa Indonesia is not the result of a deliberate government policy. It's just occurring naturally." The trend is apparently being led by well-to-do parents who can afford private school for their offspring.

OPINIONS ELSEWHERE

As English/Amglish rolls around the world, the debate about its effects is growing. In Thailand, the main complaint is the quality of teaching. Private companies that need employees fluent in the language seem to be the driving force. But many teachers are only part-time workers who may not know English well, so the net effect often merely adds to the linguistic confusion.

In other places, the main worry is the effect on native languages. In an article on the Global Envision website, several respected authorities are quoted as believing that the net result may be a strengthening—not weakening—of native tongues as a type of resistance to Amglish and a desire to preserve local culture.[40]

Singapore teacher Anne Pakir calls Singlish—a mixture of Chinese and English—a "killer language" because it has made a shambles of her efforts to teach English. On the other hand, author Salman Rushdie says "To conquer English may be to complete the process of making ourselves free."[41]

Juliane House, professor of applied linguistics at Hamburg University, adds that English can help preserve local dialects.

"Paradox as this may seem, the very spread of English can motivate speakers of other languages to insist on their own local languages for identification, for binding them emotionally to their own cultural and historical tradition."

A POLITICAL BACKLASH

At the start of the twenty-first century, the world's love affair with almost all things American turned somewhat sour. The attack on the World Trade Center towers and the Pentagon in 2001 jarred the nation into realizing that it had some serious enemies beyond the oceans which had protected the nation for so long. In a speech nine days later, President George W. Bush asked, "Why do they hate us?"

Although his word *they* seemed to refer only to the 9/11 terrorists, who were mostly Saudi members of al-Qaeda, it soon grew to include the 1998 bombers of the U.S. embassy in Kenya and anyone else who could be described as violently anti-American. A month after 9/11, a mob of Pakistanis torched a KFC restaurant in Karachi when they were blocked from venting their wrath against the local U.S. consulate. The crowd did not realize that the restaurant owner was a locally grown Colonel Sanders.

The invasion of Iraq in 2003 added to the negative feelings in much of the world. An international poll by the Pew Research Center showed that favorability ratings of the United States even in normally friendly Great Britain, for example, dropped from 83 percent before 9/11 to 58 percent after the Iraq invasion. Germans switched from 78 percent in 1999 to 45 percent at the start of the Iraq war. A Zogby survey in 2002 reported that 87 percent of Saudis had an unfavorable view of America. Other Arab nations showed similar figures.

In order to answer Bush's question, the government launched opinion polls in many parts of the world. Results showed anti-Americanism running deep in many areas. It ranged from disdain for U.S. culture as depicted on TV and in movies to dislike of government policies, particularly those involving Israel and the Palestinians, a subject often at the top of the list of international sore spots.

In response to the polls, the government chose to sidestep any possibility of reviewing or changing policies but instead launched a massive advertising campaign featuring positive images of Muslim life in the United States. However, after several countries refused to broadcast the ads and others found it ineffective, the program was canceled.

CONFLICTING MESSAGES

American businesses took the polls more to heart than average Americans did. Firms with connections overseas began to redesign their logos in order to play down the U.S. angles. The object was to save Brand America from having to retrench or rebrand itself.

But it soon became clear that the ominous signs for U.S. brands outside the country had been overstated. A 2003 survey of 105 international students at Regent's College, London, by Jami A. Fullerton of the University of North Texas agreed with a *Fortune* magazine article in 2003 that "the death of Brand America has been widely exaggerated." Fullerton also found that the students liked U.S. television, movies, and music but did not like America in general.[42]

Had it finally become smart for young people abroad to reject what their parents had considered smart now that America had become a world-class punching bag? The fact is that anti-Americanism has existed as long as America has. Britain and France are the historical witnesses to that.

FRANCHISES DEFY THE TREND

But the continued expansion and prosperity of American franchises overseas clearly demonstrate that the negative feelings about U.S. policies simply don't apply to them or their products, especially not the language that surrounds them.

American franchise operations have continued to expand internationally even while some have been retrenching at home, according to a 2009 report by Richard Gibson.[43] He reported that McDonald's had opened 286 units abroad in the most recent seven months compared to only 53 domestically during a period of tight credit.

"For overseas investors," he added, "big U.S. chains are attractive because of their brand recognition and proven profit potential. That, in turn, makes it easier to sell individual franchises in a foreign country."

To prove the point, Gibson said that Subway had opened 1,432 locations abroad in the previous five years, 202 more than were opened in the United States. And a unit of Doctor's Associates Inc. had nearly doubled its overseas presence to 8,817 outlets. Meanwhile, Curves International, a women's fitness center, had opened 612 locations abroad in a year and a half, compared to only 19 in the U.S. and Canada.

The message from abroad to Americans at the end of the first decade of the twenty-first century seemed to be, "We don't like your international policies, but we love your Big Macs, smart phones, movies, and especially your lingo."

Amglish doesn't need any promotional or advertising help.

WILL ENGLISH DOOM ITSELF?

The more the language spreads, the more some observers worry about its ultimate fate. A book published in 2010 refers to today's international English as *The Last Lingua Franca: English until the Return of Babel*.[44] Its first line reads, "The decline of English, when it begins, will not seem of great moment."

The British author, Nicholas Ostler, argues that since world English is a lingua franca, merely a language of convenience, it will be dropped without ceremony or emotion when it is no longer convenient.

Ostler is not just another Brit who is angry at what the Americans have done to his royal tongue. He is a well-respected historical linguist who knows what has happened to languages of broad convenience such as Greek, Latin, and French, to mention only three of these rare linguistic birds.

One of his two main arguments is that English is being used primarily by elites, such as tourists and business travelers with special reasons for using the language at a time when increasing democratization and rising social equality tend to bring down such languages. But the impetus for English in the world comes from all levels of society, especially middle and lower ones.

HOW OSTLER ERRS

His other main argument is that instant translation technology has reached a point where a common language will not be needed for international contacts. The only problem is that machine translation has not—and never will—reach the point where it can completely replace human translation, which can be prohibitively expensive.

In addition, Ostler commits one huge error of omission that indicates that he may have been living on the moon for the past few decades: he essentially ignores the impact of the computer, a subject that is barely mentioned in more than three hundred pages of text, with only one reference to it in the index.

He also errs in saying that the only means of communication that really matters is written or printed. The huge increase in oral discourse through computerized devices doesn't count for much in his eyes. In fact, languages change more in an oral sense than a written one.

GRADDOL'S COMPLAINT

In 2004, David Graddol, another respected British linguist, wrote an article for *Science* magazine in which he said that English no longer seemed to be the dominant language of the world. It's still important, he said, but the share of the world's population that speaks English as a native language was falling, at least in his view. He added that Chinese will continue to have the most native speakers, while English remains in second place.[45]

But his thesis does not take into account all the people who speak English as a second language. That number—an estimated 1.5 billion—is still growing and puts English far ahead of any other language. Two years later, Graddol wrote a paper for the British Council entitled *Why Global English May Mean the End of English as a Foreign Language*. In it, he acknowledged that English had become the world's primary language for international communication. "But," he said, "even as the number of English speakers expands further there are signs that the global predominance of the language may fade within the foreseeable future."

Nine years earlier, the same Graddol had issued a monumental report for the same group. It was called *The Future of*

English: A Guide to Forecasting the Popularity of the English Language in the 21st Century. On the first page, he asked, "Isn't it obvious . . . that the English language will continue to grow in popularity and influence, without the need for special study or strategic management?" His answer was a begrudging "probably yes."

Like many other Brits, he refuses to acknowledge the dominance of U.S. English or its influence on the informality of global English. At least David Crystal, author of the authoritative book *The Stories of English*, does, but only in the final, twentieth chapter.[46]

LANGUAGE OWNERS' REMORSE?

These and many other worries about the future of English appear to be essentially laments from the previous owners of the language that they had nurtured for well over 1,500 years. After such a long love affair, it is only natural to dislike what the unpredictable and irresponsible Americans have been doing to trash such an old family member.

You don't find Americans setting up big national councils to assess the future of American English. By the time such a study could be published, it would be grossly out of date. Surprisingly, there is comparatively little interest by the American media in reporting the remarkable spread of American English around the world. The subject rarely rates even a minor headline, much less a discussion on commercial radio or TV. By contrast, British newspapers and magazines eat up all language developments, and their worry beads are always out.

Nor can you find much interest in the United States in finding a name for the informal patter that is sweeping across the globe. That gives the Brits their way in naming the baby. As a result, the frequent names offered—such as *Globish* and *Panglish*—don't begin to represent the dominant U.S. role.

DISAPPEARING LANGUAGES

While Amglish is flourishing, at least half of the approximately 7,000 languages in the world are likely to die by the end of this century. Part of the reason is the rapid growth of English as the first genuine world language. A bigger factor is the massive shifting of populations from one place to another.

As the world draws closer together because of improved transportation and communication, and people move to where opportunities are greater, the need for local languages diminishes as the need for a common language grows. Areas that have lost the most languages include Asia, South America, and Australia. In the United States, the most threatened are Indian tribal dialects.

But in the case of at least one tribe, the Cherokee, the computer has given a measure of hope for the future. Surviving members of the tribe worked with Apple executives for three years to develop software for the tribe that was compatible with personal computers as well as portable versions like the iPhone, iPod, and iPad. Cherokee is now one of fifty languages supported by the Apple system. But only some 8,000 of the 300,000 tribal members still speak Cherokee.

THE THREAT OF DIGLOSSISM

There is also a growing possibility that English is becoming diglossic. The word refers to a terminal disease that can split a language into two levels: a high, intellectual version and a low or average-person version. This is what happened to ancient Greek and Latin before they eventually met their lingering deaths.

In this scenario, Amglish is lower class, while BBC English and its American counterpart are upper class. The dirty little secret is that every language faces such a prospect if it lasts long enough. Another secret is that there is no way to stop—or even slow down—the process.

Lingering within much of this history is the nostalgia factor. It is only natural for older people everywhere to bemoan the tendency of today's masses to ignore the values and traditions of yesteryear. This is especially true in countries with long pasts such as China, where the art of shadow puppetry was once popular.

When one elderly Chinese couple decided to help preserve the art, they devoted years of research to the task. They eventually opened a museum in Beijing to display their artifacts to the adoring crowds they expected. But they found little public interest in their work or the artwork itself, which tells so much about earlier Chinese culture.

Cui Yongping, the museum's curator, spelled out his lament to reporter Michael Wines: "People in China no longer learn about the things of our ancestors. What's popular now is saying *O.K.* and *McDonald's*."[47]

Nostalgia is not like it used to be. With each passing day, public interest in things past wanes a little. And the waning seems to be picking up speed just as communication itself is. To be sure, papers are still being written about Old English verse and the pivotal poetry of Geoffrey Chaucer's saucy *Canterbury Tales* in Middle English. But today's world has moved far beyond that point.

THE PERMANENCE OF CHANGE

What will happen to the large body of great English literature and history that may become increasingly ignored? And what about all the vital laws and documents that could lose their relevance and meaning as old languages fade away? You might think that the English themselves would be worried about this problem. Yet the extensive studies and reports on the future of language don't give it much attention.

No problem, say some language pioneers; such literary works will surely be saved as valuable relics of a bygone era. Broadway and Hollywood can't afford to have Shakespeare die. He is too much a part of today's entertainment world. Just to make sure, *New York Times* columnist Bob Tedeschi carries the complete works of Shakespeare on his iPhone.[48]

It's very possible that today's language ferment may create its own great works to be admired by future generations. We don't yet know what they might be. What we do know is that we can't turn back the clock. We must accept the major changes, good or bad, and learn how to cope with them.

Just think of what a single world language such as Amglish can do for all humanity. For starters, it could help unify people around the globe in a way that neither the United Nations nor any other world body has been able to do. Local languages could still serve important purposes, but a universal tongue could become a unique power for better or worse. For starters, it could reduce the chance of war and help alleviate or cure vital food and health problems.

This chapter has described how Amglish has become the first truly international language. The next chapter will focus on the major forces that have built the international power of Amglish.

From Revolution
to Tsunami

English is destined to be in the next succeeding centuries
more generally the language of the world than Latin was in
the last or French in the present age.

—John Adams, September 5, 1780

No prediction about language has been as prescient as the
one above.

If Adams could have known how people would handle the
King's English two hundred years hence, he might not have
been so optimistic. In fact, he was already peeved enough by
the quality of English in his own era. In the letter from abroad
quoted above, he urged Congress to set up an American
academy similar to ones set up earlier in France and Spain
"for refining, correcting, improving and ascertaining the
English tongue."

He explained, "It will have a happy effect upon the union
of the states to have a public standard for all persons in every
part of the continent to appeal to, both for the signification and
pronunciation of the language." Sure thing, John.

To understand where he was coming from, you have to know where he was going. This proper gentleman was headed for the White House as vice president to George Washington, then to the presidency in his own right, eventually to be followed by his son, John Quincy Adams, also as president. The only other family close to having such credentials is the Bush family, whose father-and-son presidents had somewhat different skill sets for language.

Fortunately for freely speaking Americans, the idea of federal language police has never caught fire. There have always been more than enough volunteer cops on the beat. The closest things to such an authority have been several failed attempts by Congress in recent years to designate English as the "national" language as part of an immigration-control bill. One thing blocking such a move may be the realization by some legislators that their own language might not measure up.

Ironically, the world would probably not be latching on to so much U.S.-flavored lingo today if the proper Bostonian Adams had had his way on an academy of language monitors. Look at how French eventually lost its status as the lingua franca of the world despite its head start, largely because French authorities tried so hard to fine-tune its use and fight linguistic imports instead of allowing language to evolve naturally.

EVERYTHING MORE GLOBAL

Despite his amazing prediction, Adams couldn't possibly foresee today's wired world, nor the explosion of ultrarapid communication devices that are transforming human interchanges in unprecedented, exciting ways.

He also could not have predicted the speed or amount of international travel, the immense growth of international trade, the massive migration of rural people to cities, and the worldwide shift from the agrarian society of his time to the consumer society of our own.

In recent years, Asian and Latin American countries have caught the wave, boosting their masses up the economic ladder to the level of the West and adding billions of educated participants to an international audience that craves the new communication devices and the thrill of being constantly connected to the entire globe.

For better or worse, globalization has brought nations and their populations closer together through the buying and selling process. American business has led the way by hiring foreign workers, setting up branch plants abroad, and teaching workers how to communicate in American terms. Also working to connect people have been the immense problems associated with globalization.

The quill-and-inkhorn style of Adams and other colonials has given way to a digital universe that few could have predicted even two decades ago. The contrasts are so huge that they defy detailed description here. As George W. Bush once said, "The past is over."[1] Today is for instantaneous connections from person to person regardless of distance, language, age, or other factors.

THE FAULTY TOWER OF BABEL

The Babylonian cacophony that angered God in Genesis 11 has gone international. As people become more affluent, they tend to travel more and move their homes to distant places. At the same time, millions of less affluent people are now freer to flee from unwanted conditions or to seek work outside their native village or country.

The result is a greater mixture of populations and languages than ever. Just walk down a busy street in any major city, and you will hear not only a cacophony of formal and informal language but a mixture of foreign languages, often distant ones. Mexican-born author Ilan Stavans tells about his home in New York City way back in the 1980s: "I was enthralled by the clashing voices on a regular walk in the Upper West Side: English, Spanish, Yiddish, Hebrew . . . Arabic, French, Polish, Russian, Swahili and scores of other tongues."[2] He said there was a bagel bakery, a Korean grocer, and a newsstand at the corner of 110th and Broadway with periodicals in Chinese, Hebrew, and Spanish as well as English.

In only a few generations, the United States has moved from a largely monolingual country to one that is increasingly polyglot, starting with the major cities and moving to smaller communities. Americans, who have a reputation for not knowing any foreign languages, now are hearing them next door or down the street. Suddenly the world's languages are coming to us as our own language is going to them.

The world of Stavans also helps illustrate the increasingly informal atmosphere within the nation's borders, where many nationalities, races, ages, skin colors, and dialects intermingle haphazardly in search of common ground and understanding. Today's casual lingo is a function of the growing informality of human affairs.

It's the voice of shifting styles. Clothes are an example as they drift from formal and flowery to informal, even simple and sloppy—for men, from suits, shirts, and neckties to

T-shirts and blue jeans, and for women, from dresses, skirts, and bras to pants and blouses sans bras, plus sneakers or flip-flops for shopping or moviegoing. In temperate zones, shorts are now chic all year long for many, despite occasional freezing weather.

Like words, clothes make statements. And their message today is that informality is in; get with it or get lost. Amglish is English in blue jeans.

MESSAGING AND NETWORKING

To keep current, in-people no longer merely telephone or e-mail; they message and network. They also Facebook if they are not already tweeting on Twitter or YouTubing. By mid-2010, Facebook had signed up member number 500 million. And who could guess which country is second to the United States in the number of participants? It's not China, Russia, or India; it's Indonesia.

Who could have predicted this verbal explosion? Facebook members can both friend and unfriend others with the click of a mouse. Computers are perfectly designed for such casual relationships. All it takes is to join a chat group or listserv, the latter a patented method of sending messages to many people at once. There are listservs for just about any group of people, particularly neighbors, family, or club members.

The aim is always to make networking easier and faster, for business or pleasure. The latest twist is for teachers to use social networks for posting homework assignments and conducting quizzes. Parents are also in the mix. It's a sign of the times that some have to use the World Wide Web to reach their youngsters in the next room at home.

Messaging has become a drug. The more you do, the more you want. It's also an invitation to be creative. Innovation is almost forced by the word limits and time factors. For instant messaging, the limit for a single transmission is only 160 characters. On Twitter, whether you network or micro log, your tweets must not be any longer than 140 characters.

In only five years of existence, Twitter has gained about 200 million users who generate some 150 million tweets and retweets per day. The Twitter Blog says that by March 2011, new "accounts" were being added at the rate of about 500,000 a day. We may be approaching a case of Twitterrhea because of the heavy twaffic.

CAN FACEBOOK BE UNHEALTHY?

Spending a lot of time on Facebook can lead to syphilis, according to Peter Kelly, director of public health in the Sunderland, Durham, and Teesside areas of Britain. He found a fourfold increase in the disease in areas where Facebook was most popular.[3]

Facebook has also been linked to terrorism and bullying. According to Britain's Department of Homeland Security, terrorists use the site to find new recruits and teach bomb making.

The strict limit tends to increase the attraction of the popular website and guarantees rapid and numerous postings by many people on the move. That makes it especially useful to journalists, who tend to tweet by smart phone, especially when reporting a large, complex event with other journalists. Others who seek public attention, such as bloggers, use the site to "build traffic."

The net result is that Twitter, like other social networks, plays a large—though completely casual—role in spreading Amglish, the type of English that results from such hasty, limited-length verbalizations.

DEFYING THE RULES

In the new atmosphere, there is general public reluctance to abide by traditional rules of grammar and syntax. Relaxed is the way to go, whether it is making up words or ignoring crusty standards for writing and speaking.

The making of language was once likened to the spreading of knowledge by Samuel Johnson, the famed creator of the first comprehensive dictionary of English in 1755. "Knowledge," he said, "always desires increase; it is like fire, which must first be kindled by some external agent, but which will afterwards propagate itself." He continued, "When [people] once desire to learn, they will naturally have recourse to the nearest language by which that desire can be gratified."[4]

By saying that people tend to take the "nearest language," he seemed to be saying that people tend to use the easiest way to write or speak, whether it is their national language or someone else's, and that like fire, language is constantly being consumed and altered as long as there is sufficient fuel.

Others compare the making of language and its rules of the road to Darwin's survival of the fittest. They see it as a natural evolvement of human sounds in the form of words and letters that are organized by actual practice for communicating with others. Changes in words and rules come the same way. So what is written down or prescribed as a word or rule in one era may be ignored in the next.

VERBAL CREATIONISM

The period of greatest linguistic change in all history has been the past two decades, coinciding with the blossoming of the Internet throughout the world. The computer has democratized human communication and helped to free language from the rusty concept of being correct or incorrect when speaking or writing.

Nothing is more illustrative of this than the method of adding words to the language. By tradition, big dictionaries used to wait for proof of a word's general acceptance in formal literature or speech before confirming a word or phrase for enshrinement.

But that process has been turned on its head. Now a word can gain instant popularity via the Internet or a social network. An example is Palin's word *refudiate*, which bounced from a tweet of hers to a television program and then to common use even if often used jokingly.

In the new scheme of things, serious dictionaries are not so serious. Their main purpose is no longer to certify a new entry by public acceptance but to be the first to use it in order to build traffic to the dictionary's website. In many cases, the word may be dead on arrival or have only a few hours to live.

Take the five new entries listed by Merriam-Webster Online between display ads on a random day, January 18, 2011: *huggle*, *Usian*, *gambleholic*, *recombobulate*, and *monumentation*. Who uses such words? Is it possible that M-W is trying a little too hard to titillate?

To these five not-ready-for-prime-time words was added a nearly extinct one as "the word of the day." It was *gloaming*, meaning "to glow," a term that may have peaked in Ireland in 1909 with the famous folk song, *In the Gloaming*, which M-W knew would not be on the iPod of its online visitors.

In other words, lexicography has become a big game. Traditional dictionaries have been turned into promoters of new words as lures for online ads. They desperately want to play the neologism game, which they once were supposed to police, not lead.

To be sure, not all verbal inventions are useful or lasting. But they can spice up the swirling stew, thus making language fun to use in contrast to the days when people were reluctant to speak or write freely for fear of making an embarrassing mistake.

THE COOL STATE

The pattern outside the United States is similar, with a growing feeling in non-English-speaking countries that people must use at least some modish English words, preferably American ones, in order to display just the right degree of cool among their peers.

It's all in keeping with the views of the late physician and poet Lewis Thomas that language is a living organism: "Words are the cells of language, moving the great body on legs. Language grows and evolves, leaving fossils behind. . . . Words fuse, and then mate. Hybrid words and wild varieties or compound words are the progeny."[5]

Amglish started as American slang, which formed the earliest waves of informal words and phrases to captivate international tongues. The great-great-great-granddaddy of all exportable Americanisms is a four-letter word sometimes abbreviated in two letters and loaded with many uses and meanings. Okay, so you guessed it.

There is no agreement on the exact origin of the word, but there is evidence that it goes all the way back to a 1790 handwritten court record clearly showing the letters *OK*. Another theory is that the two letters go back to an 1839 editorial in the *Boston Morning Post*. Still another version suggests that it comes from the Chocktaw Indian word *okeh*.

Whatever its origin, *OK* or *okay* is still considered the most common American word in the world. It has withstood the test of time and is still used frequently in conversations by native

speakers as well as by those who were not born with English on their tongue.

Thousands of other American words have also gone international. And many have become integral parts of daily conversations in nearly every country. Linguist Leslie Dunton-Downer lists thirty common English/American words used often in other countries. Of the thirty, I counted twenty-eight that were in global circulation well before the computer age.[6] They include *bank, business, bye, check, cocktail, cookie, credit card, deluxe, disco, film, free, fun, hello, jazz, job, made* (as in "made in China"), *parking, penthouse, relax, robot, safari, SAT, shampoo, star, stop, stress, taxi,* and *T-shirt.*

Anglicisms in world use but not necessarily from the United States also go deep into history. According to Jon Winokur's 1995 book *Je Ne Sais What?* such expressions started in 1833

GLOBAL ENGLISH MONGRELS

Following are sample words from lishes, the combinations of English and other languages around the world:

Chinglish: *t-xue* for T-shirt in the Latin alphabet of Mandarin Chinese

Finglish: *oh my god,* as spoken by the natives of Helsinki

Franglish: *les chicken nuggets,* usually spoken at the Paris McDonald's

Hinglish: *postwalla* for mailman in Hindi in India

Iranglish: *elastic loaves,* the official term for pizza in Iranian Farsi

Italglish: *fastforwardare,* a verb heard in Rome along with *stoppare*

Japlish: *sekushii* for the English word *sexy* in Japan

Paklish: *bakpaki* for a suicide bomber with backpack in Pakistan

Runglish: *ized cyawfeh* for iced coffee in Moscow

Singlish: *dis visiting guy* spoken in Singapore

with the naming of *Le Jockey Club* in Paree. Hundreds of English words have been "borrowed" either intact from English or altered to look French.

In the "borrowed" category are words that have been imported by the French without change, including the following ones that start with the letter *b*: *bacon, badge, ballast, barman, best seller, bitter, blazer, bluff, bookmaker, boomer, booster, boss, boycott, brainstorm, brain trust, break, budget, bull, bulldozer, bun, bungalow, bunker, bus,* and *business*. In the "altered" category are *le vocabulaire* and *trafic*.[7]

COMPUTER DRIVEN

The main driver of language changes is the personal computer, the marvels of which are now in the hands of an estimated 2 billion people, nearly one-third of the globe's population.

The computer has shrunken much of the world to a lighted screen that furnishes a common ground for people everywhere to communicate with each other at a faster pace than seems possible. In little more than two decades of mass usage, the device has

- destroyed the fax machine and rendered many mailrooms obsolete,
- rendered printed dictionaries and language guides almost irrelevant,
- nearly eliminated telephone directories and printed maps,
- reduced traffic at libraries,
- altered commuter traffic because of offices in homes, and
- slashed the audience for broadcast and printed news.

This ingenious device has also shown a remarkable ability to affect personal life by making it easier to blame a machine for writing errors, to avoid the trouble of writing personal letters, and to reduce or eliminate child care expenses. The computer also has a few personal downsides, including the ability to

- help increase body fat beyond what's needed to survive the winter,
- raise or lower sex drive (usually located next to the hard drive), and
- distract workers from doing their jobs.

SPIN-OFFS AND FALLOFFS

At the same time, the computer and its progeny have been undergoing sweeping changes. Not only are they being constantly upgraded and enhanced with new apps (applications), such as constantly available music and weather reports, but they are being reshaped into an amazing collection of spin-offs, including cell (mobile) phones, laptops, netbooks, and assorted "tablets," like Amazon's Kindle and Barnes & Noble's Nook.

Smart phones are essentially pocket computers with as many as 300,000 free or paid apps to choose from along with connections to Facebook, e-mail, texting, music, games, a camera, a calculator, and GPS travel guidance—your keys to the world.

So let us pity William Powers, the author of *Hamlet's Blackberry*, who fell off a sailboat with his phone and thereby became "unreachable"—the worst of all predicaments in the computer era—for more than an hour, almost the equivalent of an eon in oldspeak.[8]

In the equivalent of a millisecond in global history, humans have attained a level of connectivity that could not even be dreamed of a few decades ago, and at speeds equally unimaginable.

But to communicate does not necessarily mean to understand, especially where different languages are involved. Translation can help, but it can be slow, inefficient, and costly, despite enormous technical improvements made in recent years. To reach understanding, a common language is better than the most uncommon translator.

In fact, without actually trying to construct such a verbal meeting ground for the world, the creators of today's data transmitters have been unconsciously doing just that. Simply making so many devices so useful and enticing sets the stage for a common language.

A PHONE FOR EVERY BODY

If you build a revolutionary communication device, don't be surprised if there is a human stampede to get it and use it. Recall the international scramble in 2007 to get one of the first Apple iPhones with third-generation (3G) powers.

Even a decade ago, nobody could have predicted that the number of mobile phones in the world would grow to 5 billion by the end of 2010, as reported by the UN telecommunications agency.[9] Nor could many people have predicted the ready ability to have a conversation almost anywhere in the world for free or to take part in a conference from your home or office.

Before phones became so intelligent and companionable, there was also no handy, quick, and effective way for productive workers and others to do research, do business, or oth-

LOVERS MADE PHONELESS IN INDIA

In the state of Uttar Pradesh, India, authorities have gone so far as to take cell phones from single women in order to prevent unarranged marriages. AFP, a worldwide news service, reported that two dozen couples from different castes had eloped after coordinating their escape by mobile phone.[10]

erwise communicate in such an efficient manner even while walking the dog or waiting in a checkout line.

The mere presence of so many phones—approximately one for every adult in the world—is a powerful incentive for them to be used—and used to the max. It also sets the stage for a common language at a time when such an idea never made better sense.

The drift toward a single language is especially appealing to diplomats, tourists, business executives, doctors, songwriters,

EVEN POOR FARMERS NEED CELL PHONES

One reason for the huge number of cell phone users is the aggressive sales tactics of manufacturers. Most of them have focused on the affluent end of the social scale. But Nokia, the Finnish phone company, has tapped into the pool of indigent farmers in India, where only 7 percent of the population has access to the Internet.

Nokia's subsidiary aim is to supply prices and other market data to growers in rural areas where such information is hard to get. One farmer, for example, reportedly learned that he could sell his onions more profitably in another city as a result of data he received by text. For the service, Nokia charged him only $1.35 per month. The firm says more than 6 million people had signed up for the service in India, Indonesia, and China by November 2010. Next market: Nigeria.[11]

publishers, lawyers, drug dealers, ponzi schemers, and just about anyone else seeking a broad audience.

Cell phones have also given many millions of people who had no land lines the ability to communicate internationally. Donald Terry, an international consultant, says that in Kenya, for example, where there were never more than a few land lines, most people went directly to cell phones. Now almost everyone there has one, not only for conversations but for money transfers.[12]

But as a continent, Africa has lagged far behind the rest of the world in connecting to the Internet largely because of the lack of reliable electricity.

PHONE FRENZIES

The younger you are, the more likely you will spend nearly all your waking hours talking to or texting friends and acquaintances. It is not unusual now for high school students to send or receive 3,000 messages a month, the equivalent of 100 per day.

One fourteen-year-old girl in Redwood City, California, reportedly sends and receives about 27,000 texts a month, nearly 1,000 a day.[13] She boasts that she can text one friend while talking to another on the phone, no doubt while doing her homework.

If a youngster is not part of a family phone plan, the costs can mount up rapidly. The parents of one high school girl in the Washington, D.C., area wound up with a month's phone bill of nearly a thousand dollars before they realized they could save a bundle on a family plan.

THUMBS UP FOR A CHAMPION TEXTER

Who's the best texter in the world? In the United States?

Nobody really knows, but fifteen-year-old Kate Moore of Iowa beat out twenty other contestants in the U.S. National Texting Championship in June 2009 by sending 14,000 messages a month, according to *Discover* magazine.[14] She won $50,000, and she did it while blindfolded—like the other contestants.

The magazine's news release unfairly wondered "whether she was sacrificing human contact and, possibly, communication skills, all for the sake of her glowing cell phone screen." Of course, the winner denied the accusation and maintained that she, like, keeps good grades and is otherwise normal. She said texting helps her prepare for exams because it can help her look back at things to review. So there, editor.

A HEALTH WARNING

A decade ago, the cell phone world was abuzz with fears that excessive use could cause brain cancer. Evidence was scattered and inconclusive since it was based on individual cases. So cell phone makers and doctors got together for a conclusive study designed to settle the question, with 13,000 participants involved.

When the results were announced in May 2010, they showed that those who conducted the study should have telephoned each other more. The main finding was inconclusive. As Elisabeth Cardis, the study leader in Barcelona, explained, "This was a very complex study, and results were very difficult to interpret because of a number of methodological issues." Sort of like a giant busy signal among the study participants.

But what about the busy digit that does all the texting? Sending so many text messages every day can make even a tough thumb rather sore. Names for the problem include RSS (repetitive stress syndrome), "Blackberry Thumb," and "teentexting tendonitis."

The cure? Outside of quitting or reducing phone time, both obvious nonstarters, the best treatment, according to C. Forrest McDowell, Ph.D., is Solomon's Seal, an herbal plant with tiny white flowers that is also said to cure other ailments. However, as everyone knows, digital diarrhea is incurable, especially among the young.

THE PRESSURE TO INNOVATE

Another major issue is the necessity that most texting be done with the letters and numbers on the telephone dial. Since there are three or four letters on eight of the numbered buttons, it means that each number must be touched one or more times to indicate which letter or number is intended by the caller.

For example, if you want to tell a good friend to "get lost," you must hit the number 4 once, the number 3 twice, and the number 8 once merely to send the word "get"; then follow the same procedure for the second word. Phones like Google's Android and Apple's iPhone make texting slightly less difficult with their full but miniature keyboards.

CALL HER DOCTOR OF TEXTING

Let's all sing praises for Dr. Caroline Tagg for parlaying her craze for txtg into a doctorate in the subject at Birmingham U.[15] She endured some 11,000 text messages containing 190,000 words—not much for a teenager—sent by 235 people before finding that people text in the same way they speak, using unnecessary words and fuzzy grammar. Her 80,000-word thesis concluded that there is more to texting than just abbreviations.

In a comment to the press, she dipped into a little informal English: "People use playful manipulation and metaphors. It is a playful language. Not only are they quite creative, it is also quite expressive." Will the next doctorate at BU be in Amglish?

In order to keep within these tight parameters, many users have devised an elaborate array of abbreviations, acronyms, emoticons, numbers, and codes to shorten thoughts to fit.

"Love you" comes out as *luv u* in English, *tq* for *te quier* in Spanish, and *ta* for *ti amo* in Italian.

Such fractionalized lingo inspired author Norman Silver to turn poetical:

> In the old old days
> B4 there were mobile fones
> How cud a boy eva meet
> A person of the oppsite gender
> & even if they cud get acquainted
> Wivout a mobile fone
> How cud they ch@
> Each uvver up[16]

A sample IM might say "AFAICT YIM is NBD but it left me ROFL with TMI BTW Im near a POP so GBFN ILU." Translation: "As far as I can tell, your instant message is no big deal, but it left me rolling on the floor laughing with too much info. By the way, I'm near a parent on the prowl, so goodbye for now. I love you." The obvious response: "ILU2."

Some of the better-known acronyms, abbreviations, and shorteners are going oral. It is increasingly common to hear even a geezer respond to a joke by spelling out the letters *L-O-L* or *O-M-G*, while younger people often combine the first acronym into one word, which is now creeping into some dictionaries and books.

THE SCANDAL DIVERSION

With computerized communication becoming so intimate, it is only natural that it might sometimes become a personal embarrassment. After the news about Tiger Woods' auto accident

in 2009, rumors of his extramarital exploits began to leak out via voice messages. Soon there were at least twelve women claiming to have privately entertained the much-admired golf star. He eventually admitted getting off course.

Less than a year afterward, the cell phone network went viral again when another big sports star, Brett Favre, the off-and-on-again quarterback for the Minnesota Vikings, sent nude photographs of himself by phone to a beauty queen also employed by the Vikings. The transmissions that were leaked to the media didn't end his career, but they came close. The two celebrated cases hinted at what many less prominent people may be doing with their own phones for kicks.

MERCHANTS ON MOBILES

It is inevitable that wherever there is an efficient communications system, there will be advertisers and promoters to take advantage of it. And as long as there is a possible sale, there will be someone to help facilitate it.

One major facilitator is MotionPoint Corporation. It claims that it can provide websites covering as much as 83 percent of the 2 billion phones connected to the Internet. It lists the top ten international languages in order starting with English, followed by Chinese, Spanish, Japanese, Portuguese, German, Arabic, French, Russian, and Korean.

As a result, customers of Papa John's, for example, can place their order by mobile phone all over the world. So if you are flying to Bahrain and you need a pizza when you arrive, you can call ahead and have your order placed in Arabic—or English. MotionPoint is expanding its Spanish mobile service to other industries such as health care, insurance, and banking. For a company like Best Buy, the global approach includes text messaging, microsites, and apps in Spanish.[17]

THE ULTIMATE TRANSLATOR?

If you are a tourist in a foreign country, you can throw away your tourist guide and pocket dictionary. That's what the ads might soon say about free and low-priced apps for smart phones that automatically translate nearly two dozen languages.

All you need to do is speak into the phone, and your words will be instantly turned into the language of your choice on the screen, which you can then show to the person with whom you are speaking. Other apps can actually speak foreign languages by turning your own words into the language of your choice.

But there are a few bugs that might be expected with such new technology. One is that the translation can be too rapid for comprehension. Another is that the first two pioneer phones, Android and iPhone, require a network connection, which can lead to some big charges. Then, of course, there is the big chance that the meaning will not be clear.

There are similar programs for personal computers. Google is trying to develop a technology that will work as an instant oral translator. But there is no way that any of these devices can achieve perfection because of the subtle differences in meaning that can occur in all languages.

In the absence of a perfect translator, Amglish stands ready to help. It's far from perfect, but it can get the job done.

FROM SNAIL MAIL TO E-MAIL

No computer function has been more effective in promoting Amglish in recent years than e-mail. This freewheeling system of communicating is also ideal for experimenting with language. Its versatility allows users not only to send and receive messages instantly but to add pictures and documents almost without limit.

In less than two decades of widespread use, e-mail has obliterated more outmoded language rules than all the Bushes and Palins combined. It has also left the U.S. Postal Service's "snail mail" with even larger deficits because of the changes e-mail has made in personal communications.

Perhaps its most significant accomplishment has been to turn traditional patterns of personal correspondence upside down. The art of letter writing used to be taught in school, but no course is necessary to learn how to communicate via e-mail. All you need to know is how to use the computer keyboard and connect it to the Internet.

This type of e-freedom is so exhilarating that many users disregard all they ever learned about writing—or common courtesy. In the typical e-mail, there are few, if any, capital letters, punctuation marks, or similar impediments to even informal writing. In such an atmosphere, many people act as if they can let it all hang out. They don't realize that everything they write is etched permanently on the hard drive and can be resurrected later.

THE HIRSCHFELD VIRUS

Such e-mail practices brought a mock warning from *Washington Post* writer Bob Hirschfeld, when he wrote that an attack of the deadly Strunkenwhite virus would automatically return e-mails to senders if they committed any grammatical or spelling errors. He added, "The virus is causing something akin to panic throughout corporate America."[18]

Actually, there was no panic in the business world because everyone knows what to expect with e-mail. Taking liberties with spelling and grammar are no longer considered abnormal or surprising. Indeed, many e-mailers may no longer be able to tell what a grammatical or spelling error looks like.

A bigger problem for most people is spam, including the unwanted offers from Nigerians to make you rich quick if you will only send them your PIN numbers and bank account passwords. A further downside is what might be called e-mail fatigue, the increasing habit of not immediately responding to messages and then losing sight of them for good on the screen.

What makes e-mailing and texting such perfect laboratories for developing new language is not only their sense of freedom from rules but the virtual absence of editing. This can lead naturally to misunderstandings, but they pale in comparison to the challenge of finding meaning in a collection of jumbled letters, numbers, and spaces.

The language of chat rooms is often even more informal and disjointed than in e-mail. That's because participants don't usually know each other except through the Internet and because of the speed with which messages are exchanged. When you're up to such speed, who needs to worry about syntax and similar details?

A NEW STUDY AREA?

Are all of these lowercase letters, missing periods, misspellings, casual grammar, and other departures from formal English signs of a new type of language being formed?

The answer is yes, and David Crystal is already on the case with a 2011 book entitled *Internet Linguistics: A Student Guide*. It focuses on text messaging, e-mailing, chat groups, virtual worlds, and the World Wide Web as new areas of study for linguists.

The book describes the growing use of these services by teachers for giving assignments, conducting classroom discussions, providing student access to libraries from off campus, and presenting guest speakers via Skype, the online international phone service. The tech term for all this is "computer-mediated communication," or CMC.

Also included in the above term is the entire emerging photosphere, including photo blogs, video logs, audio blogs, and blog blogs. Blogs are called "the beginning of a new stage in the evolution of written language." There also are RPGs (role-playing games), MUDs (multiuser domains), and the creative use of punctuation, like *!?!?!?!?!?!?*, emoticons, and asterisks.

Promoters of this new type of language don't seem to realize that all this already has a name. It's Amglish.

CRITICS WEIGH IN

Many a parent or teacher has privately bemoaned the state of such language arts and has wondered what the long-range effects might be on young people and their ability to go to college and get decent jobs.

One prominent critic is James Billington, the librarian of Congress. He says he sees "creeping inarticulateness, the demise of the basic unit of human thought—the sentence. If the sentence croaks, so will critical thought. The chronicling of history. Storytelling itself." After using two nonsentences, he used a few real ones to explain:

> The words "community" and "communicate" come from the
> same root word. It logically follows that greater communication
> would lead to greater community, would bring us all together.
> . . . The Internet revolution creates new possibilities for people to
> be in touch with others, but it could also lead to a gobbledygook
> language without sentences and punctuation and paragraphs—
> and with less understanding of the world and its meaning.[19]

Billington is one of very few public authorities who dare to dis the language of young people. Most teachers and professors tend to be either afraid to be quoted or are unusually inarticulate, probably because they don't want to lose any remaining rapport they still have with students.

However, Ben Yagoda, a professor of English at the University of Delaware, is not afraid to speak out. He says today's students seem brighter than earlier ones, but their ability to write clearly has declined greatly in recent years. Referring to bloggery and text messaging, he adds, "The things that suffer the most are spelling and punctuation."[20]

TEENS NOT SO CRITICAL

On the surface, today's teens don't seem to see anything amiss according to a 2007 survey by Pew Internet & American Life Project and the National Commission on Writing. Of those surveyed, 60 percent said they did not consider texting the same as writing, nor did they believe that technology negatively influenced the quality of their writing.

Yet nearly two-thirds admitted that the texting style—such as acronyms like *LOL*—slips into their schoolwork. Nevertheless, an overwhelming 86 percent said good writing is important to success in life.

These two findings seem to indicate that many teens are doing more texting than they would like, perhaps because so many of their peers are doing it. They are apparently being swept along by a fear of being labeled "uncool" or "nerdy" by their peers.

According to the survey, parents were more positive than their children with regard to whether computers make for better writers and more creative, better communicators. They were also less negative than their children with regard to the effects of computers on spelling and grammar. But how much do parents really know about what is happening? And how much is wishful thinking?

A government essay test conducted in 2008 by the National Assessment of Educational Progress indicated that only one-third of the nation's eighth-graders and only one-quarter of high school seniors showed proficiency in writing. These results clearly pleased Amanda P. Avallone, vice chair of the federal testing program involved. She declared, "I am happy to report, paraphrasing Mark Twain, that the death of writing has been greatly exaggerated."

Her hidden message seemed to be, "Hey, we are trying to keep a stiff upper lip, but considering the times we live in and the pressures on today's kids, these test results are better than we expected. So let's all go out for pizza and beer."

WIRED FOR DISTRACTION

It's not hard to find reasons for the slipping ability to write sparkling prose. One reason is distractions. Youngsters find it extremely difficult to resist the flood of inventions to speed up communications and make them more intimate.

GROWING UP DIGITAL, WIRED FOR DISTRACTION—that's the way the *New York Times* headlined its front-page analysis of the situation in Redwood City, located in California's Silicon Valley.[21] The story said the lure of computers and cell phones, particularly texting, is beating out the desire for an education, not to mention the need for physical exercise.

At the same time, these students and their parents are among other Americans at the forefront of fashioning the new world language. Without realizing it, they are helping to create today's substitute for formal English.

The process of spawning a new language used to average about 1,600 years, according to linguist Robin Dunbar.[22] Now

TOO MANY BLACKBERRYS

Ariana Huffington, the founder of the popular *Huffington Post* blog, is proof that too many Blackberrys can be harmful to your health. She was trying to keep up with three of them when she passed out from exhaustion and broke her cheekbone.

She says her first therapy was to charge her batteries in a separate room from where she slept. She then decided to go comparatively naked telephonically by dispensing with the third phone.

Alas, the divorce didn't work. She says she's back to three intimate companions and risking turning the other cheek into shreds.

it takes only a tiny fraction of that total, just enough for the computer world to lay the groundwork.

LIKE A REVOLUTION

By 2004, Crystal concluded that such massive changes in language truly amounted to a "revolution" because there was "so little continuity with previous communicative behavior."[23] By that he meant that for the first time you could now have a "conversation" by texting or e-mailing without actually seeing or hearing the other person involved. And for the first time you could have more than one conversation simultaneously, with the response time now anywhere from less than a minute to a month or more.

The fact that there were now more users of English as a second language than as a first language was, to Crystal, also "without precedent." The ratio of second-language speakers to first-tier ones had reached the astounding figure of three to one. Never had any language attained such dominance.

Crystal also found that "English as a *lingua franca* was developing a new linguistic character," due not only to the massive input from the United States but from the regional dialects of Australia, India, South Africa, and other countries. He called the result "a hybrid without a name."[24]

The hybrid has become even more prominent in non-English-speaking countries, which stretch far from Europe where English is clearly the second language for nearly everybody. The new lingo has been especially welcomed in countries like China and Japan, where the contrast in language structure is greatest.

Cutting across all these factors is the generational one: the huge linguistic gap between younger and older people of all nationalities. The former tend to experiment and seek change; the latter tend to resist change and stick with the status quo. The youth factor is a major force in spreading English to non-English-speaking countries.

TOWARD A WORLD TONGUE

Throughout modern world history, languages followed explorers and traders. The linguistic seeds especially helped spread Spanish, English, French, Dutch, Chinese, and Portuguese to their colonies.

But these trading centers generally remained isolated linguistically from each other, despite some interactions in pidgin dialects. No one country or language dominated the world.

For several centuries, French was considered the lingua franca, the language of international diplomacy. But that began to change at the end of World War I when the Versailles Peace Treaty was written in both French and English, largely because of the huge contribution to victory provided by Britain and the United States.

Since World War II, American English has been the common language for almost every international activity, whether it be diplomacy, trade, advertising, technology, music, film, broadcasting, science, navigation, travel, or sports.

SIGNS OF UNITY

A major side effect of the war was a worldwide quest for some way to avoid another world war. With American leadership, the United Nations was born in 1945, the same year the war ended.

Since then, the UN has grown in member states from only a few dozen to nearly two hundred, including nearly every sovereign state in the world. So has the number and scope of its activities. The UN has also inspired the growth of numerous nongovernmental organizations (NGOs) for many international purposes. They include groups promoting trade, preventing hunger, improving general health, promoting education, and stamping out disease.

The very existence of so many international organizations and programs has added pressure for a single language that would allow more efficient communication, not only for the UN and its satellite arms, but also among nations. Although the UN has six official languages, English has dominated open discussions and official reports from the start.

The ultimate test of a language is its power to absorb the inflections, dialects, accents, and other irregularities that go with the territory. The attraction of English perhaps lies more in its informal state than its formal one. After all, it is easier to learn a few fundamentals that allow more people to communicate on a basic level. This may be the secret to why English seems so adaptable and flexible. Since the advent of the computer, it has also been more available than any other language.

TERROR GROUPS CHOOSE ENGLISH

Even international terrorists have joined the parade. Allies of Osama bin Laden have learned to send messages in English and have apparently enticed a number of recruits in English via the Internet. One example is Nidal Hassan, who killed thirteen people at Fort Hood after becoming friendly by computer with Ayman al-Zawahiri, an Egyptian-born cleric who was close to bin Laden before the latter was killed.

Al-Qaeda has even launched an online magazine in English called *Inspire*.[25] The first edition was somewhat amateurish, with instructions for making "a bomb in the kitchen of your mom," an article on "Mujahedeen 101," and a lesson in sending and receiving encrypted messages.

Apparently a virus interrupted most of the pages. Reporter Jeremy W. Peters wrote that the problem "could have been the work of hackers, possibly working for the United States government."

English has become the chief foreign language taught in the schools of more than one hundred countries, though the quality varies considerably from nation to nation and from classroom to classroom. English is even replacing French in North African countries. In Tunisia, where a dictator was toppled in early 2011, the government is now requiring it in primary schools.

DID JESUS SPEAK ENGLISH?

Although the above question may sound ridiculous, it keeps popping up in real American places like Texas.

Persistent reports indicate that a feisty female governor of that state named "Ma" (for Miriam A.) Ferguson once declared, "If the King's English was good enough for Jesus Christ, it's good enough for the children of Texas." She was reportedly facing pressure to allow Spanish to be taught in state schools in the 1920s.

Frequent repetition has kept the concept alive.

In China, each child is required to take English for the first nine years of school. But the quality of teaching varies considerably, largely because so many teachers are former students who were never exposed to the authentic sounds, accents, and mannerisms, which differ so much from Mandarin, the national language of China. Japan begins English lessons at five years of age. Even Mongolia has plans to be bilingual in English.

OTHER LANGUAGES LOSING STATUS

While interest in learning English continues to expand, interest in studying foreign languages has been waning and wavering in the two major bases of English, Britain and the United States.

The contrast appears greater in the island nation, according to a study by the European Commission in 2005. It said that only 30 percent of Britons could converse in any foreign language, while only 10 percent spoke a language other than English at home. The results lent support to the popular view of the Englishman abroad who thinks he can be understood by raising his voice and repeating himself.

In response to criticism, the British government issued a study the next year ordering that foreign language study be required up to age fourteen, beginning in 2010. But it disappointed many educators and business leaders by leaving in place an earlier decision that no language study be required after that age.

In the United States, a 2010 survey of 3,200 public schools by the Center for Applied Linguistics showed that thousands of schools had stopped teaching foreign languages, mostly because of the economic recession. Hardest hit were traditional courses in French, German, and Russian, while courses in Chinese and Arabic were growing the fastest. Spanish, the most popular foreign language, was found in 93 percent of middle and high schools, largely because of the huge influx of Latino immigrants in recent decades.

The 465,000-student State University of New York (SUNY) decided in 2010 to end all majors in French, Italian, Russian, and the classics, Latin and Greek. Dozens of other universities are doing the same.

According to the Modern Language Association, the proportion of foreign language courses to all college courses in the United States stood at 8.6 percent in 2009, roughly half of what it was in 1965.[26] The U.S. is said to be the only major country where a student can complete high school or college without studying any foreign language.

Also in 2009, the European Commission issued a forlorn plea for help in filling a "serious shortage" of interpreters in nearly every language. It bemoaned "the belief that being able to speak English is enough for international contacts, both for one's work and for one's personal or social life."

WHY NOT MAJOR IN JAVA?

Reacting to SUNY's cutbacks in foreign language study, French philosopher Jean-Luc Nancy of the University of Strasbourg wrote, "To choose between eliminating French or philosophy . . . what a fabulous choice! Should one take out the liver or the lung? . . . Perhaps it would be wise to introduce in their place, as requirements, certain computer languages like Java [or] what is displayed on our advertising billboards and on stock exchange monitors."[27]

Meanwhile, English has been recognized as an official language in some seventy nations, with more than 2 billion total population.[28] Countries where English has an official status but is not the native tongue include Ghana, India, Nigeria, and Pakistan.

MORE LIKE A TSUNAMI

Under the rapidly changing circumstances, Crystal's use of the word *revolution* to indicate a revolt against the status quo seems outdated only seven years later.

What is happening might be better described as a verbal tsunami that is sweeping across the globe and disrupting—if not enriching—nearly all languages in its path. No shore is unwashed by the waves of new words and new styles of writing and speaking.

Clearly the main catalyst in the past two decades has been the Internet, which has been dominated from the beginning by the United States with its tech terms and slang. In the first wave of websites, over 85 percent were U.S. based. That percentage has dropped considerably since then because of wider usage of local languages, but American English is still the international favorite.

This dominance has forced computer users throughout the world to learn enough American English to get around the Internet efficiently. The pace has been so fast that translators for local and national languages have been unable to keep up in many areas, further forcing people to deal with English terms, whether they want to or not.

WHAT'S IN A NAME?

But what to call the evolving international language? In Britain, where language changes arouse much more interest than in the United States, close observers have favored terms like *Panglish* or *Worldlish* to represent the broad reach of English.

In addition, there are various engineered languages, including Esperanto, Basic English, Globish, Simplified English,

Plain English, and General Service List (GSL). Esperanto was invented by L. L. Zamenhof in 1887 and was officially recognized by UNESCO in 1954 as a mixture of several European languages. Basic English was created and trademarked by Charles Kay Ogden and gained some popularity after World War II. It is based on 850 key words.

Globish was created and trademarked in 1998 by Jean-Paul Nerriere, a French former IBM executive, who selected 1,500 words as a basic vocabulary. He sells books, including his own 2009 book entitled *Globish the World Over*, containing rules and lessons. In 2010, Robert McCrum, an editor at the London *Observer*, chose the proprietary word *Globish* as the title of his book describing the intermingling of English with other languages. His book praises Nerriere without specifically endorsing the learning materials he sells.

A Simplified English was developed for the aerospace industry with rules restricting sentences to no more than twenty words, and "noun clusters" to no more than three words. Plain English is attributed to Sir Ernest Arthur Gowers, a British civil servant and author of *The Complete Plain Words*. GSL is a list of some 2,000 words selected by Michael West in 1953 as enough to understand about 90 percent of colloquial speech.

Happily for humanity, none of these artificial lingos have caught on widely, though many an English teacher has probably exhorted her pupils with lowercase pleas to write in simple, plain, basic English.

THE CASE FOR AMGLISH

As for a nonproprietary name for the new lingo, there have been many suggestions, but all—including Global English,

Panglish, and Worldlish—originate in Britain, the country most worried about the future of its mother tongue.

But not one reflects the dominance of informal American English in the evolving international lingo. Yet in his book McCrum admits that the evolving language "is heavily influenced by linguistic and cultural developments in the United States.[29]

Googling the word *Amglish* in February 2011 brought nothing relevant except a single entry in the online *Unword Dictionary*, which said Amglish is "spoken by the majority of people in the United States, and indeed some young people in the United Kingdom." Some individual Brits have acknowledged online that the word *Amglish* better reflects the facts on the ground in their own country than other names.

The word *Amglish* even has an ancestral quality to it. It is only a tiny blip away from *Anglish*, the first spelling of English when it separated itself from Germanic and Nordic tribal mutterings in the fifth century.

Perhaps it's time for professional linguists and the international community to finally recognize the leading role of informal American English in creating the first genuine, easily usable lingua franca.

Whatever name eventually sticks to the verbal mélange, citizens of the world have been ready for years to lap up any language that works for them in their efforts to communicate with other people in the world.

This chapter has described how communications technology, globalization, and other factors have made the world so receptive to an informal international language. The next chapter describes more than two dozen international "lishes," the combinations of national languages with English.

The Lishes of Amglish

FEEL YOURSELF AT HOME.

—A welcome sign in Amsterdam's Schiphol Airport

The sign quoted above is typical of the Amglish found all over the world. It shows the humorous result when a non-native speaker of English tries to use the language in a public way without making sure that the meaning is what the writer intended. The Dutch are particularly adept at this type of composition.

The sign is just one of many language mixtures seen or heard in today's global cacophony. Words and syllables from one or more languages are imported into another language, often resulting in a mixture that is humorous, hard to understand, or both.

Hilarious errors on signs and directions in pseudo-English have become so common around the world, especially in China, that they have inspired a large number of fictional works rather than accurate reporting, especially on the Internet. The possibilities are endless.

175

But the genuine blending of languages with each other is even more fascinating because it is predominantly a natural process that can lead in many directions. One of the sharpest observers of this phenom is Jug Suraiya, a satirist for the *Times of India*. In 1999, he wrote about how English itself is often mixed in his own country:

> Like an indefatigable bindlestiff (tramp, US) or a haggler (itinerant pedlar, West Indian), the English language roams the world, selling its wares and pinching words from other languages, leaving behind a brood of linguistic offspring: Amglish (American English), Windlish (West Indian) and our very own Hinglish.

He proceeds to list various verbal blends popular in India: *footfall* (number of people entering a shop during a certain time), *croning* (a celebration to honor an older woman), and *ohnosecond* (the moment you realize you've made a mistake by pressing the wrong computer button.[1]

This chapter is a summary of linguistic mixtures, with names that show a blending of English with various national languages, many of which have already been described to some extent earlier in this book. Not included, with one exception, are local and regional dialects or creoles, such as the French-Spanish creole of Louisiana, which are such thorough mergers of languages that the sources of words are not easily recognizable. The exception is Pennsylvania Dutch.

Spanglish is an example of a well-known "lish." A resident of Madrid may use it to *parquear* his car near a *Starbucks* so he can *surfear* the Web on his *laptop*. Likewise, a native of Paris might use a bit of pure Frenglish to buy *les chicken nuggets* at a local McDonald's, while a Roman signorina plans to *stoppare* at an *Internet cafe* to *fastforwardare* her computer *input*.

Most of the lishes described here have been mentioned earlier in this book but without the additional details that follow. All are part of the extended Amglish family.

A MIXED BAG

It is not always easy to categorize each type of verbal mixture because it may be a combination of portmanteaus, loan words, or other types of merging one language with another. It could also be like the airport sign, whose writer didn't know which words to borrow and where they fitted.

But most of the traffic in lishes is oral, often making spelling more of a guessing game than it already is. To help with that, we are already seeing the first wave of books devoted to individual lishes, such as Ilan Stavans's book on Spanglish, which contains a large glossary.

The lishes described in this chapter are among the more prominent of many. The sheer number and the speed with which they have circled the globe without much press notice clearly indicate that Amglish—in all its forms—is destined to become even more of an international language.

There isn't room in a small book to describe all these linguistic mongrels. Perhaps such a compilation is another book, even an encyclopedia. But no story about today's international lingua franca would be complete without citing this extensive, ongoing, unique development. There are perhaps dozens more in the process of forming. See www.amglish.org.

Of course all languages are constantly rubbing up against others and absorbing or discarding volatile parts. What's different today is the acceleration of the process and the everready presence of American English.

INTO THE GRAND MIXER

The process resembles a huge Cuisinart with all languages constantly spinning around to separate the useful parts from the others. No one can adjust the speed, control the ingredients, or stop the process. Eventually new languages and dialects are formed, while others slide away.

In fact, it is becoming common to hear people frequently shift from one language or dialect to another and then back again in the same conversation. Tony Badran, a Lebanese-American, told me that his family and friends in Lebanon normally use three languages at once: Arabic, French, and English.[2] They might say "Hi" or "Hello" and then shift to French and Arabic, and maybe an *OK*. Or they might use a word or two containing parts of all three languages. The net result is Amglish because of the presence of American English.

Most of the lishes described here are new in a historical sense, since they are essentially products of America's worldwide hegemony and cultural invasion since World War II. But three—Hinglish, Spanglish, and Singlish—are in a class by themselves as the oldest.

Hinglish is a mixture of English and Hindi. It goes back to 1617 when the British West Indies Company received permission to trade with India. As trade expanded, the British sent military forces there and eventually obtained control of the country. That control extended to the imposition of the English language in government and the educational system of the country.

THE CULTURE FACTOR

In the latter part of the twentieth century, however, American cultural invaders, mostly from Hollywood, started to put an

American accent on the common parlance. The massive out-sourcing of U.S. jobs in recent decades has added further to American influence.

The Spanish portion of Spanglish in the Western Hemisphere was seeded by Spanish explorers and a notable Italian, Christopher Columbus, when they set foot in North America beginning in the fifteenth century. But it wasn't until the early eighteenth century that English was added to the mix when the eastern colonies began to expand into the far reaches of the continent.

The Spanish discoveries eventually led to successive waves of conquistadores who moved from South and Central America into the western parts of what would become the United States. Their descendants are still on the move into almost every community in the country as their Spanish language constantly sinks deeper into American English.

Singlish, the third oldest lish, emerged in the early nineteenth century when British traders landed in Singapore, the tiny nation that has always been a major port for international merchants. The term began with a mixture of British English, Malay, Hokkien, Tamil, and Cantonese.

It wasn't until 1965, when the British ended 146 years of colonial rule there, that Hollywood films and TV shows ramped up their incursion in the tiny nation. Many well-to-do families in Singapore have added to the American influence by sending their children to schools in the United States.

EMERGING LISHES

New lishes are being formed so fast and in so many places that it is impossible to keep current with them. For example, young Tibetans are in the process of creating their own merger of

Tibetan and English, according to Andrew Grant, an American teacher of English in the Volunteers in Asia program. He adds that for them, sound is far more important than spelling.

He says he had to give each student an American name because it was so difficult to remember their native names, the sounds of which did not resemble anything in English. He also says a typical Tibetan male knows four languages: Tibetan, Chinese, his own dialect, and English. Most of their English apparently comes from American TV shows.

The only continent lagging in a strong English presence is Africa. But that is starting to change in a hurry, particularly since the 2011 uprisings in Tunisia, Libya, Egypt, and other places.

Tunisia has become the center of a movement—English for Development in Africa—to promote English as a first foreign language for all parts of Africa that do not already have it. For many North Africans who are native speakers of Arabic, that means switching from French to English as a second language.

Following are summaries, in alphabetical order, of some of the various lishes, including more details about the three oldest ones and others mentioned elsewhere in the book.

ARABLISH/ARABISH

Arablish (or Arabish) is one of the most exciting branches of Amglish because until recently there was no easy way to turn Arabic into English and vice versa without a time-consuming translation process.

Now, there are Web-based devices that allow a writer of English, for example, to automatically type an Anglicized form of Arabic that can then be transcribed automatically into Arabic. This is not strictly a natural blending of Arabic and English but a halfway point between the two that uses English letters and Arabic numbers. The numbers are used to represent Arabic images that have no counterparts in English.

In Arablish, the word *English* becomes *Engliziya*, *yes* becomes *Na3am*, *no* becomes *La*, *hello* becomes *Mar7aban*, *goodbye* becomes *ma3a alsalamah*, *I don't know* becomes *La a3rif*, the number one becomes *wa7id*, two is *ethnan*, three is *thalatha*, four is *arba3ah*, and five is *5amsah*. So "Hello, what's your name please? I don't understand," could be transliterated into something like "madr7aban ma esmok arjook la afham."

Arablish is increasingly used on the Internet and in other types of international communications, such as advertisements by multinational firms. In addition, there is an Arabic chat alphabet for encoding Arabic into Arablish in order to send SMS messages over the Internet or by cell phone.

CHINGLISH

English has become a national craze in China despite the difficult learning process and growing opposition from the government.

As stated earlier, children must take lessons in English through the ninth grade. But phonetics can be difficult, since most Chinese cannot pronounce certain English letters. In the Cantonese dialect, for example, the letters *l* and *n* are considered interchangeable. So the cartoon character Snoopy can become "Sloopy," and Emily's name may sound like "Eminy." The *th* sound is nonexistent in Chinese, often causing the word *three* to emerge as "shree." The English letter *v* is often pronounced like a *w*.

Many other problems stem from the built-in defects and ir-regularities of English. The result is a conglomeration of errors in sound and spelling. Mistakes are often attributed to think-ing in Chinese while writing or speaking in English.

FOR A LAUGH, PUT AMGLISH ON A SIGN

When it comes to lettering signs throughout much of the world, the fractured language of Amglish is often worth a hearty laugh. The humor is so great that it has spawned many fabrications, especially on the Internet. The following words are from photographs taken by American Alex Michaelson in China:

- THE TROLLEY HAS NO BRAKE. PLEASE KEEP IT OUT OF REACH OF CHILDREN. PLEASE DON'T GO DOWNSTAIRS WITH TROLLY.
- PLEASE DIAL 68346000 IF YOU FIND THE WATER PROBLEM.
- STAR RATED TOILET.

A sign on the wall of Silk Street Market, a shopping center in Beijing with 1,700 vendors, warns clerks against using certain "Forbidden Words" on customers. They include *You are crazy*, *Shit*, *Just go away*, and *Stupid guys*.

Food labels can also be giggly sometimes because of trans-literating problems. Samples include a label on a jar of plums saying, "Hey, so delicious, let us try it fast," and a package of crackers labeled "Burned Meat Biscuits."

A supermarket sign meant to draw customers to a delicious display of food items read, "It is gluttonous to come quickly." Another item was labeled "Fried Enema." A public sign warn-ing hikers of danger said, "Please do not climbing." Another common sign at the end of a tour or pathway says "Welcome Again" instead of "Come Again."

One bank offered two signs, one for "cash withdrawing," which made sense, and one that didn't, "cash recycling." And a clothing store offered some large-size clothes unbelievably labeled "Fatso" and "Lard Bucket."

Sign Police Get Mixed Results

With the Olympics looming in 2008, the government set up the Commission for the Management of Language Use to eliminate the most embarrassing signs before the crowds appeared. With some six hundred volunteers, the commission claimed that it fixed more than 10,000 signs. Among those affected was a sign for the Dongda Anus Hospital. It was changed to Dongda Proctology Hospital. And Racist Park was renamed Minorities Park.[3]

Young Chinese are very computer oriented and like to show off the latest American words acquired from the Internet or television. According to Beijing native Yi Han, almost any new U.S. product, technology, or idea is immediately accepted by its English name or acronym, such as *MP3*, *iPod*, *Wi-Fi*, and *DVD*, or transliterated into pinyin, which uses Western letters for Chinese characters.

Some transliterations can sound quite ingenious. Han cites *bo ke* for blog; *ji in* for gene (literally, "basic code"); *kao bei* for copy; *hei ke* for hacker (literally, "black guest"); *fen si* for baseball fans (literally, "thin rice noodles that wrap around other food"); and *sai bai wei* for Subway, the restaurant chain (literally, "compete with hundreds of tastes"). Matthew Michaelson, an American expert in Chinese literature, adds the Mandarin word for T-shirt: *t-xue*, pronounced "tee shir."

DANGLISH

English is Denmark's first foreign language and is spoken by nearly everybody in this tiny country. Dorte Lonsmann of Roskilde University says her research on the computer game culture there in 2007 indicated that young Danes frequently code-switch from Danish to English.[4]

Lawrence White, a native Brit who runs a language translation and learning center in Denmark, says English there is frequently influenced by the rules of Danish itself, often resulting in good but slightly odd English. For example, instead of asking what something looks like, a Dane is likely to say, "How does it look like?" because the same question in Danish starts with the word for *how*.

Meanwhile, many English words are finding a place in Danish, such as *deadline*, *computer*, and *chance*. White adds that universities and business schools in Denmark conduct many international courses in English, and that accompanying textbooks are available only in English.[5]

DENGLISH

Denglish, or Denglisch, as the Germans spell it, has been extremely popular in Germany for years. It is exemplified especially in technical terms, such as "rebooting a computer because the software crashed," a phrase that comes out as "*rebooten den computer weil die software gecrasht ist.*"

Young Germans especially like American terms, which they often transliterate. For example, they may refer to *coole events* or use gansta rap terms such as *phat*, which they spell "fett."

Wikipedia describes a whole category of English words that are given meanings in German that differ from their meanings in English. Among such words, with their German meaning in parentheses, are *dressman* (male model), *drive-in* (drive-through) *evergreen* (a golden oldie), *fitness studio* (gym), *oldtimer* (classic car), *parking* (parking garage or lot), *smoking* (tuxedo or dinner jacket), *street worker* (social worker), *timer* (calendar or appointment book), *trampen* (hitchhiking), and *wellness-hotel* (spa).

Free-flowing writing often adds spice to Denglish. In his blog on what he calls Germanglish, Johannes Ernst describes an invitation from VDI, an engineering organization, to a conference. It listed one speaker's topic as "Fright traffic and passanger services between different interests." On the subject of visiting a Mercedes plant, the brochure recommended, "Please register for the visitation in the registration form attached."[6]

Pennsylvania Dutch

An earlier type of language mongrel called Pennsylvania Dutch has been spoken for centuries by some 200,000 German-Americans in Pennsylvania and a few other states. The name of the dialect comes from the German word *Deutsch*. Here are some samples of this type of Amglish:

- Throw father down the stairs his hat.
- Father ain't so good; his eatin's gone away and he don't look so good in the face either.
- Ve get too soon oldt und too late schmart.
- Go out and tie the dog loose and don't forget to outen the light.

DUNGLISH

Dunglish has been piling up for many years in tiny Holland, this mostly flat land of dikes and canals. It's a kind of middle English—or should we say "muddle"—that speak and write the Dutch in a manner malaprop. They know the English words but have the trouble putting them on the traditional order.

A blogger on WTForum!! explains, "I question me off, or blogging in English would pull more readers on. You see, everybody cans English. Not as fluid as me naturally, but that speaks. For me, writing in English is a little egg, because English knows no secrets for me. In fact, my English is even good as my Netherlands. But make yourself no worries, because when you don't snap a word or a sentence, can you always ask for outlay in the comments. O, in that fall, try to use correct English grammar and gaming."[7]

Schiphol Airport in Amsterdam has been called a hub of Dunglish with its signs, such as the one at the beginning of this chapter and another from the dunglish.nl website, saying, "Need Your Baby Some Rest? Visit Our Special Baby Room."

FINGLISH

In Finland, the home of Nokia and other large international business firms, the influence of English has been huge despite major dissimilarities in the two languages.

Since English has become the principal language of international firms, it is natural that English terms would also drift into everyday conversations between Finns. In the past, they have borrowed more words from nearby nations, especially Sweden and Russia. But that has changed in recent decades.

According to Feodor Bratenkov, a business executive residing in the country, the natives may lapse into "Oh No," the name of a Finnish-made movie; "What's up?"; or when surprised, "Oh my god." Finns also transliterate English computer terms into their own language. An example is the word for a mouse click: *klikkaa*.

Many Finns migrated to the United States from the 1880s to the 1920s, mostly to the upper Midwest and to mill towns in New England. Their descendants like to put the letter *i* at the end of English words. Examples are: *elkki* (elk), *jarri* (a jar), *lemoni* (lemon), *resortti* (resort), *toiletti* (toilet), and *klerkki* (clerk). The suffix *-ata* is also popular, as shown by the words *kompleinata* (complain) and *taipata* (type). A heart attack comes out *haartatakki*, and to be satisfied is *satosfai*.

FRENGLISH/FRANGLAIS

Despite substantial government fines for egregious use of foreign terms, French conversations and public media are replete with unchanged English or bastardized English words. Recent examples of the latter include *le drug store*, *le fast food*, *le software*, and my all-time favorite, *les chicken nuggets*. Others include *je suis tired*, *je ne care pas*, *le marketing*, *le shampooing*, *un parking*, and *supercool*.

Since 1975, use of such words has been against French law. Among other words banned in France are *la call girl*, *le cocktail*, *le dancing*, *le showbiz*, and *le weekend sexy*, just the words most needed by American tourists looking for a good time with *beaucoup* dollars to spend and a limited knowledge of *Français*.

In August 2006, the country's Culture Ministry added *e-mail* to thousands of already banned English words and proposed a fine of up to $1,800 per violation. But the campaign has done little or nothing to stop *e-mail* from appearing—with or without the hyphen—in either the sent file or inbox.

The main reason for the bans, of course, is to help preserve what's left of *la culture française*, but nothing the French government can do will stop *la marche de l'Amglish*. It has too much *big mo*, as they say in Paree. To show just how bilingual they are, many French retailers invent English-looking words to get the attention of shoppers. Two of most interesting are *relooking* for a makeover and *destockage* for clearance sale.

Most of the Amglish words in France get started in the media because of the natives' efforts to keep current. However, serious French journalists covering the world and national politics tend to stick to the language formalities. A prominent exception for the news pages of Paris's *Le Monde* for years has been *think tank*. The Academy's tank is obviously leaking.

Except for the main newspaper sections, just about anything goes. A random perusal of *Le Monde* revealed this Amglish headline over a story about tennis player Aravane Rezai: "*TENNIS: forfait a l'open GDF, Rezai avait 'besoin d'un break.'*"

A random perusal of *L'Express*, the newsweekly, turned up this potpourri: *La Fashion Week parisienne en 50 street looks*. *Le Point*, still another newsweekly, contains sections called "*Mode et design*" and "*Tech et net*." A story about a rising Spanish star was headlined: *la success story d'asak adic*.[8]

GIBBERLISH

Gibberlish is written or spoken Gibberish with an Amglish tinge. It usually means a meaningless collection of words created by incompetence or accident, similar to a massive malapropism.

But there is always a chance of a hidden meaning lurking in the verbal underbrush. So it cannot always be cavalierly dismissed or derided. The most common habitats of Gibberlish are e-mailing and texting. The disease can usually be identified by a mysterious string of letters and numbers that seems to be understandable but is not.

Once again, George W. Bush has set the standard, this time for Gibberlish. He did so on December 13, 2005, in answer to a question from a woman in the audience about his plan to privatize Social Security. He said in part,

> Because the—all which is on the table begins to address the big cost drivers. For example, how benefits are calculated, for example, is on the table. Whether or not benefits rise based upon wage increases or price increases. There's a series of parts of the formula that are being considered. And when you couple that, those different cost drivers, affecting those—changing those with personal accounts, the idea is to get what has been promised more likely to be—or closer delivered to that has been promised.

GREEKLISH

There are two types of Greeklish. One is a technical linguistic transliteration of the Cyrillic alphabet of Greek into English letters and vice versa. Various websites contain converters that will automatically do the job. But because of the un-Roman shape of some Greek characters, the Arabic numbers 3, 4, and 8 are substituted for them.

This type of artificial language hasn't gone over well among the natives. In 2004, a few Greek websites threatened to ban any such variations of Greek as a danger to the future of demotic (Modern) Greek. Other critics contended that the Roman letters did not do justice to the Greek ones they replaced.

The other form of Greeklish is the substitution of common English words for Greek ones in newspapers and magazines. Irene Grossman, a Greek teacher in the Washington, D.C., area, spotted many such words in a random perusal of the Athens daily, *Kathimerini*, for February 14, 2011. English words were used not only for sections of the paper, such as Real Estate, Articles, Newsletter, and Good Life, but for other parts of the paper as well. Among the verbal mixes was the English word *test* spelled in Greek letters.

HINGLISH

India is a land of many tongues with no one language other than possibly English serving the whole nation. Until recent decades, Hindi had the most speakers, and British English served as a *lingua franca* (bridge language) for the nation.

More recently, Indians have switched to American accents in order to handle the hundreds of thousands of service jobs outsourced by U.S. corporations.

Hinglish is a mix of Hindi and English, with an Indian accent that sometimes renders it difficult for native English speakers to fully understand. Examples include *badmash* (naughty), *timepass* (spare time), and *fundoo*, a version of *cool*.

Much of Hinglish comes from advertising agencies. The result is lots of mixed messages, such as *"Thanda mani Coke, Hungry kya?"* and *"What your bahana is?"* Coke's slogan in India is *"Life ho to aisi"* (Life should be like this).

In 2006, Baljinder K. Mahal, a teacher in Derby, England, created a dictionary entitled *The Queen's Hinglish: How to Speak Pukka*. It features lots of verbal blends of Hindi, Urdu, and Punjab, lingos that add to the English already in Hinglish. Among the book's Hinglish words are *airdash* (to travel by plane), *would-be* (fiancé or fiancée), *eye-teasing* (sexual harassment of women in public), *postwalla* (postal worker), *freshie* (new immigrant), and *filmi* (drama).

Indian movies have become powerful forces in spreading English. Although Hindi is the main language of Bollywood films from Mumbai, a growing amount of dialogue is in English, particularly in song lyrics. Bollywood, a portmanteau of *Bombay* (the former Mumbai) and *Hollywood*, has been especially instrumental in spreading English internationally since the 1970s when India became the world's largest film producer.

Back in the States, some Americans who have lost jobs to India have coined the word *Bangalore*, as in "I've been Bangalored." Translation: "My job has been sent to Bangalore," a hub of such business in India.

HUNGLISH

This is a combination of English and Hungarian, often in the same sentence. An example from a blog called "The Great Hungarian Experiment" is the following: "Szia Emily! Thank you a konyvet! You are very aranyos! Elkezdtem to read it, I like it nagyon. Koszi again! Take care." Translation: "Hi Emily, thank you for the book. You are wonderful. I started to read it, I like it greatly. Thanks again! Take care."

Nick Grossman, a Hungarian native living in the United States, says English words appear regularly in Hungarian news reports. Sample words (including a misspelling) found in January 2011 included *monitoring, parlament, sport,* and *forum.*

ITALGLISH/ITALISH

Not surprisingly, there has been a massive influx of Amglish in Italy, the father of Latin and the great-granddaddy of many English words. By now, Greek, Latin, English, and Italian have become so intertwined that it is hard to tell which part comes from which language or all of them. If you asked a native if that's true, the likely answer now would be "yes, yes," not "*si, si.*"

The latest wave is a brash blend of Italian and English words, such as *stoppare, fastforwardare, monitorizzare,* and *editare.* Then there are *shopping, la pop art, footing* (for running), and *basket* (for basketball). To share is *sherare* instead of that mouthful *condividere.* As a result, it would not be surprising to hear an Italian say, "*Ego shopping per la pop art . . .*"

The newspaper word for help-wanted ads has become *miojob.* A random front page of the daily *La Repubblica* had more than three dozen English words, including *foto*, *graphic novel*, *star control*, *shopping*, *news*, *style*, *torture*, *design*, *amnesty*, *showroom*, *sport*, *forum*, *topless*, *single*, *sexy*, *username*, *password*, *help*, *online*, *blog*, and *podcast*. Many advertisers assume that all Italians can read English.

JANGLISH/JAPANGLISH

According to T. Kaori Kitao, professor of art history at Swarthmore College, Japan is unique among nations for the prominence it gives to English, especially the American variety, in the country's culture. Much of the influence no doubt comes from the occupation of the country by Americans after World War II.

Alexander Michaelson says newspapers and magazines often use English-derived words, also known as *wasei eigo*, written in katakana, a phonetic syllabary that represents foreign words in Japanese. He added that English words are particularly common in Japanese fashion magazines, such as *Glamour* and *Miss*. For those who don't know Japanese, there are computer plug-in translators on search engines to render everything into English.

The Japanese are especially ingenious at creating English words for their own use. Samples from whatjapanthinks.com include *power harassment* (bullying) and *paper driver* (a person who has a license but no car).

In katakana, the English word *sensation* becomes *senseshon*, *charming* becomes *chamingu*, *shampoo* becomes *shanpu*, *sexy* becomes *sekushi*, *beer* becomes *biru*, and a *baseball out* and *strikeout* become *besuboru auto* and *sutraiku-auto*, with a strong accent on the final syllables of the last two terms. The letters *AV*, which normally mean *audiovisual*, refer also to *adult video* (porn) in Japan.

Michaelson adds *Makudonarudo* for McDonald's (or just plain *Makku*), *Sutaba* for *Starbucks*, and *dokuta-sutoppu* (pronounced "doctor stop") for a doctor's order to stop drinking or eating so much. Many English words are conveyed to young Japanese through music lyrics, which can be either in English or Japanese, with a healthy amount of *wasei eigo*.

J-rock refers to Japanese rock music, and Ellegarden is the name of a punk rock band that often uses English words as lyrics. One such song is titled *Windy Day*. Another is *Santa Claus*, which is sung partly in Japanese, partly in English.

KONGLISH

Konglish describes several types of Korean and English mixtures. One is anglicized Korean with Latin letters of the alphabet. Examples of such words are: *ge-im* for *game*, *bi-di-o* for *video*, *syo-ping* for *shopping*, *cho-ko-lit* for *chocolate*, *bol-pen* for *ballpoint pen*, *a-I-seu-keu-rim* for *ice cream*, and *haem-beo-geo* for *hamburger*.

Another type of Konglish is transmogrified English with results that are often hilarious. For example, a sign for a traditional barbecue comes out as LEGITIMATE BARBECUE. Another is a sign in a store window saying "Family Photo," with a line that reads, "Memorize Your Marriage."[9]

Koreans also like to shorten long words in ways that even Americans themselves might envy. For example, an office-hotel complex boils down to *officetel*, a word processor becomes *wo-pro*, and a digital camera becomes *di-ca*.

Koreans are especially clever at fabricating words with English letters such as *skinship*, which means physical contact between two or more people that is not necessarily sexual. Another is *hwai-ting*, pronounced like *fighting* (with heavy

emphasis on the last syllable), a term for an all-purpose type of cheering or encouragement.

Korea Times columnist Jon Huer, who supplied the above examples, says Koreans "are ingenious in creating all sorts of combinations, subtractions, modifications, distortions . . . to suit their purpose. There are literally hundreds of such Konglish inventions and creations in use."

MANGLISH

At first, Manglish and Singlish seem to be essentially the same, but Manglish is said to represent more of a Malaysian influence in the ports of Malacca and Penang. Unlike Singlish, it doesn't follow any grammatical rules. As a result, some of its variations are not understandable to people speaking other versions. It might be said, therefore, that English is more mangled in Manglish than in Singlish.

According to Wikipedia, Manglish grew out of street lingo in Malaya, while English prevailed in British administrative offices. In Malaysia, the Chinese tend to speak Malay when conversing with other Chinese, but they speak English when they converse with other Chinese in Singapore.

PAKLISH

English is one of two official languages of Pakistan. It is the language of government, the courts, and the media, although Urdu, the national language, has more speakers. Most large daily papers are published in English or have English editions. English is also taught in school, where much of the instruction in other courses is also in English. Almost all Pakistanis know at least some English words.

Like India, Pakistan first learned English from its early British occupiers, which explains the predominant British accent. But it is changing to American, largely because of the substantial influence of U.S. films and TV, and more recently the presence of many American military and security personnel.

However, English words are sometimes hard to understand because of native accents and frequent misspellings, this according to the Business Rules Forum, an international organization seeking to make business firms more effective. An item on its site says, "The chief reason for the misspellings is because [forum] members love to parody Pakistanis."

If a word is accidentally misspelled in a leading Pakistani newspaper or journal, forum members are likely to quickly pick up the mistake and adopt it as their own. An example is the common phrase "going for the jugular vein." It's more likely to come out as "jaguar vein."

Among English terms, according to various sources, are *shopper*, not as a person but as a bag; *open/close*, with the meaning of turning something on or off; *get no lift* (receive no attention or assistance); *tight* in the sense of high quality; and being *out of station* (being out of town).

As for Paklish, Arif Khan, a writer for www.netvert.biz, says many Pakistanis think in Urdu and speak in English. He says an example of the mixture would occur if a young Pakistani phoned his American girlfriend and said, "My heart was wanting *kay* I talk with you." (*Kay* in Urdu means *that*.)

Khan cites another example: a notice to a bank customer about a withdrawal of seventy-five rupees: "For issuing new cheque book we charge RS. 75/–. Yeh amount aap kay account mien debit kar dee gai thee." At that point, a nervous customer might want to look for another bank and check the bank balance.

PORTUGLISH/PORGLISH

This is a lingo spoken (and written) not only in Portugal and Brazil but in areas of the United States by heirs of Portuguese immigrants going back hundreds of years. The areas include parts of California, Hawaii, and eastern Massachusetts.

Maria Angela Loguercio Bouskela, a native Brazilian doctor, says that in the last ten years English has become much more popular with Brazilians as they move up the economic ladder in tandem with the country's economy. Travel to the United States has also increased substantially.[10]

Examples of Portuglish words that are similar to Spanglish are *apontamento* (appointment), *atachar* (attach), *comutar* (commute), *deletar* (delete), *escore* (score), *friza* (freezer), *inicializar* (initialize), *resetar* (reset), and *scanear* (scan).

However, the government passed a law in 1999 that forbids the use of foreign expressions in public documents. It was a reaction to the frequent use of American English terms such as *boom*, *delivery*, *fast food*, *personal banking*, *rock*, *site*, *striptease*, and *videotape*.

Portuguese Impressions, a blog on the WordPress website, provides additional examples of written Portuglish by exchange students from Brazil.

RUNGLISH

For nearly three centuries, Russians took the advice of Czar Peter the Great to "write everything in the Russian language, not making use of foreign words and terms."

But everything changed after the fall of communism and the Soviet Union in the late 1980s. Suddenly the country became caught in the headlights of Western culture and business. At the time, Russians had few linguistic terms to deal with the rest of the world, so they simply transliterated English terms into Russian.

Feodor Bratenkov, a native of St. Petersburg, reports that "the number of Americanisms became so enormous that one needs many pages to write all of them."[11] They include such terms as *offshore*, *roam*, *site*, *file*, *mixer*, *toaster*, *roast*, *shaker*, *bowling*, *skateboard*, *snowboard*, *biker*, *fitness*, *security*, *broker*, *teenager*, *parking*, *microvan*, *showroom*, *prime time*, *blockbuster*, and *multiplex*.

Although Runglish (a.k.a. Ringlish or Russlish) has been kicked around for years by humorists, the first practical use of it was claimed by Russian astronaut Sergei Krikalyov, who reported that the mixture of Russian and English was used by him and his fellow astronauts in 2000 at the International Space Station. A similar scene occurs in Arthur C. Clarke's novel, *2010: Odyssey Two*, about a spaceship crew that started a "Stamp Out Russlish" drive.[12]

Brief Backlash

By 2007, Russian leaders had apparently had their fill of Americanisms. They declared it "the Year of the Russian Language," hoping to stop young Russians from picking up and passing on words mostly from MTV, the international music channel. But Yuri Prokhorov, chief of the Russian State Institute of Foreign Languages, admitted at the time that there was no way to stop such a trend. A bigger problem, he added, was the failure of many Russians to use their own language properly.

By 2011, Bratenkov reported that Runglish had become even more prevalent. He said a random review of the Russian news agency *news.ru.com* revealed a headline saying in phonetic Russian that a supermarket chain named OKAY had shut down all its supermarkets in St. Petersburg. The story included Cyrillic spellings of *supermarket*, *retailer*, and *top manager*.

He says Runglish is especially prominent in the public relations field. If you know Cyrillic letters but don't know Russian, you might be able to determine the meaning of many current words for such things as positive PR and negative PR.[13]

A version of Runglish lives in Brighton Beach, Brooklyn, where Russian-Americans frequently get away from either Russian or English with such terms as *kool*, *koka-kola*, and *friendessi* (girlfriends), words that they undoubtedly get from television and movies. Worth noting is the Runglish word for Xerox copy: *kserokopirovat*.

SINGLISH

Singlish, the third oldest lish, continues to thrive today but with its original British flavor increasingly spiced with American terms. Most young people in Singapore reportedly consider it their primary language, while others use it as a second language.

As described at the beginning of this chapter, Singlish is a mixture of many languages, reflecting the cosmopolitan nature of the tiny country, where public signs are often written in three or four languages. Although Singlish borrows many English terms, it is not easily understood by native English speakers because of the bizarre mixture of words and the accents given them.

In fact, there are various versions of Singlish itself. In the simplest combination of Standard English and Singlish, the sentence, "This person's Singlish is very good" comes across as "Dis guy Singlish damn powerful one lah." In a more colloquial version, the same sentence comes out, "Dis guy Singrish si beh powerful sia. It can be damn confusing to dis visiting guy."

In 2000, the government started a "Speak Good English" movement in an effort to reduce the use of Singlish. But Singlish has reportedly continued to proliferate on radio and television, reflecting its increased popularity with the general public, especially comedians. Humor writer Sylvia Toh Paik Choo has written several books about it, including a glossary called *Pasar Patois*.

SPANGLISH

Spanglish has been spoken in the United States for centuries. But never has it had such currency as now when federal and state governments are struggling to control the persistent flow of Latinos into the country.

As a result, some American newspapers in English are starting to run sections and columns in Spanish or Spanglish. One of the latter appears in *The New Mexican*, a daily in Santa Fe, New Mexico, under the title Growing Up Spanglish. The author, Larry Torres, writes it in such way that a person without any knowledge of Spanish can understand it.

Spanglish comes in many forms, depending on the country of origin. It ranges from the Cubonics spoken by Cuban-Americans, to the Nuyorican spoken in New York by Puerto Ricans, to the Dominicanish from Dominican Republic and the Spanglish spoken by Mexican-Americans in East Los Angeles, or *Istlos*, as denizens of the area pronounce it.

Spanglish also thrives in other Spanish-speaking countries, particularly in Latin America. Even the British living in Argentina are said to speak it. American Spanglish even has its purists who claim that the Tex-Mex common in Texas is not Spanglish because it is a variety of Mexican Spanish, nor is the Ladino spoken in parts of New Mexico, for the same reason. But not to worry; they surely qualify as Amglish.

Meanwhile, American words and phrases are increasingly creeping into conversations among Spanish-Americans, while many Spanish words are becoming Americanized. Latinos often ask for a *Kleenex* rather than a *panuelo*, and they *butear* (boot up) their computer in order to *surfear* (surf) the Web. If a mistake is made, they *deletear* it. Typical Spanglish words include *colid* for caller ID, *for-yun-key* for a 401(k) account, and of course the famous *grincar* for a green card.

In Spain, the home of pure Spanish, there is broad contempt for the mixture of Spanish and English as the language of the poor. Yet Spanglish can be seen there in restaurant menus, literature, and heard in popular music lyrics, especially rock, hip-hop, and salsa groups.

SWENGLISH

English has a strong presence in Sweden, especially in the sports, computing, and business worlds. The results often are amusing examples of Swenglish, which can take the form of English with a heavy Swedish accent and grammar, or Swedish with many English words.

Many mistakes come from grammatical differences in the two languages, as well as from literal translations of Swedish idioms. Examples of Swenglish words are *briefa* (to brief someone) and *maila* (to e-mail someone).

English is widely used at the university level and is often used even when there is a Swedish alternative. Like many other nationalities, Swedes have a habit of using many terms from American pop culture, such as "Shit happens."

TAGLISH

Taglish is halfway between English and Tagalog, the main language of the Philippines. The mixture is becoming the country's lingua franca and is especially common in the metro Manila area. Its main advantage is said to be its comparative brevity compared to Tagalog or Filipino words, which are becoming less familiar. Filipino is a liberalized form of Tagalog.

The following examples show what happens when English creeps into local languages:

A question in English asking "Can you explain it to me?" becomes "Maaaring ipaunawa mo sa akin?" in Tagalog but "Maaaring i-explain?" in Taglish.

And a question asking, "Have you finished your homework?" becomes "Natapos mo na ba yung homework/assignment mo?" in Taglish. By the same token, a statement in English, "Please call the driver" becomes "Pakitawag ang driver" or "Paki-call ang driver."

Taglish is also said to be more suitable for instant messaging and is used by Filipinos who live in English-speaking countries.

TIBETLISH

Tibet is not so remote anymore. According to students there who have learned some English, many young people speak a mixture that sounds very much like the language young Americans speak.

Tsemdo Thar, a Tibetan who learned English in the Volunteers in Asia program based in San Francisco, cites such common terms as *bye-bye, okay, cool, wow, hello, hey man, yahoo, gmail, laptop, MP3, DVD, iPod, Mac, and Apple,* plus the normal array of four-letter words and other obscenities.[14]

Tsomo Faith, another Tibetan new to English, says the local word for credit card is *ca,* boots are *bol tu,* and Jeep is *jeep.*

TURKLISH

Turklish is almost entirely a creature of American films, TV programs, music, and fashions. According to American Serdar Tonbul, young people in Turkey like to buy Converse sneakers at twice the price of competing brands mostly because of the American name. English words like *operation* and *communication* are often preferred by young people over Turkish terms. American slang and obscenities are also becoming increasingly common.

Tonbul lists many words that are mixtures of Turkish and English, including *cet* (pronounced like the English word it means, *chat*), *sorvir* (server), *terapi* (therapy), *enteresan* (interesting), *makina* (machine), *atac* (attach), and *adres* (address).

VIETLISH/VIETGLISH/VINISH

This mixture of English and Vietnamese is primarily a product of the Vietnam War, which brought so many unwelcome things to Vietnam by American military might.

One of the biggest leftovers from the war is the fragmentary English spoken by so many Vietnamese either in their own country or abroad. Wikipedia lists the following examples of such English words in Vietnamese: *tivi* (television), *xi cang dan* (scandal), *xe tang* (tank), *soc* (emotional shock), and *mat* (mad or crazy).

YIDLISH/YIDDISH

Here is a language that goes back to the tenth century in the Ashkenazi culture and yet is as current as the newest Americanisms. It is essentially a melding of German and Hebrew.

You don't have to be Jewish to delight in Yiddish terms such as *chutzpah, kibitz, klutz, kvetch, maven, mensch, noodge, nosh, nudnik* (and *nogudnik*), *schlemiel, schlep, schlock, schmo, schmuck, schnoz,* and *tukhus*.

You also don't have to be Jewish to mix Yiddish terms into English. Such words are so widely understood that there is no need to fabricate new words in order to speak Yidlish, a term to indicate the use of Yiddish by native English speakers without the proper Yiddish pronunciation.

This chapter has described some of the so-called lishes that have been formed from the merger of English and various languages around the world. You should now be sufficiently prepared for the next chapter, which offers ten lessons in how to master Amglish.

Ten Easy Lessons

Communicating with other people should be easy, painless, and shameless.

Yet many Americans have been routinely intimidated—even terrorized at times—by parents, teachers, and others for even the slightest departures from rules and standards formulated centuries ago. It is time for everybody to relax and let language evolve naturally within every person without threats or intimidations

Silent resentment against ancient strictures has simmered long enough in English-speaking countries, especially the United States. For Americans, the rebellion against formal English started with the overall resistance by the colonies against nearly everything British.

The resistance has reflected the restless, free-swinging character of Americans embodied in the revolutionaries of colonial times through successive waves of ambitious immigrants imbued with a natural pioneer spirit.

As this book shows, there have been many individual attempts to break out of the mold that is still sometimes labeled the Queen's English. Among the leading language rebels have been authors, musicians, lexicographers, teachers, humorists, and advertisers, as well as ordinary people, especially young ones.

Almost all have been seeking ways to simplify a language too complex and formal for the time and make it easier and more enjoyable to use.

The result is today's Amglish, an informal mixture of American English and other languages. It is the largely undirected product of free spirits altering the structure and style of the language. The new lingo is shaking off outmoded precepts and idiosyncrasies as it silently invites all to hop aboard, have fun, and be subtly altered in the process.

Unlike the rules of formal English, the rules of Amglish are unwritten and as fluid as society itself. While its basic structure remains relatively stable, new words as well as grammar and syntax are steadily reshaping it. The resulting mishmash is being embraced enthusiastically almost everywhere.

Along the way, Amglish is developing its own *modus operandi* (MO) in order to be more broadly understood. The following lessons are designed to acquaint anyone who hasn't kept current with what has been happening. Amglish's emerging standards appear to be intelligently designed by nature, like all living creatures.

Unlike the rules of formal English, the rules of Amglish are flexible and made to be broken as conditions change. All but the last of the ten lessons should be taken with at least one grain of salt followed by a suitable chaser. The tenth should be taken to heart, especially by young people.

It's time to play the language game for all it's worth.

LESSON ONE: GO WITH THE FLOW

The main point of this lesson is to relax when trying to communicate with others.

Let the words tumble out without worrying about where or how they will land, and don't fret about whether you are forming a complete sentence or something quite different. If you are in the writing mode, don't sweat over your words before sending them. You will break the casual image that goes with Amglish.

Life is too short to worry about making errors in language. It is also too short to pass judgment on possible grammatical lapses or questionable wording by other people. To learn Amglish is to tolerate all verbal sounds and shapes and to accept them without question.

The key is to reach understanding through communication. If that means writing without capital letters or proper grammar, so be it. Lowercase letters on a keyboard can build rapport with people as well as save the time it takes to use the shift key, unless of course you are writing to a college admissions office or a prospective employer. Just think of the hours—possibly even years—that poet e. e. cummings gained for other things by avoiding the shift key on his typewriter.

Amglish lovers should also not be awed by centuries-old dilemmas that force people to choose between *further* and *farther*, *lay* and *lie*, *that* and *which*, *who* and *whom*, and other dilemmas. Scarcely anybody today—even with an advanced degree—has a firm grip on such relics. Nor have several American presidents despite their receiving superior education.

Among other problems that still reverberate in classrooms and books is whether to use a preposition—a word like *of* or *for*—at the end of a sentence. For centuries there was a strict prohibition against it. But the rule abruptly died when Winston Churchill became agitated enough to dismiss the problem by saying, "That's the sort of pedantry up with which I will not put."

Thanks to him and others, the language establishment has finally agreed—though not unanimously or openly—that such a rule is no longer necessary. The practical answer comes down to whether ending a sentence with a preposition gets the point across.

Meanwhile, similar anachronisms are disappearing in the new linguistic atmosphere.

So let the good times roll with rules and standards that are easy to live with.

LESSON TWO: BETTER TO PHONE THAN WRITE

This lesson is designed to encourage you to maximize your dependence on phones and films so you don't have to waste time and effort reading and writing things, learning stuff, and thinking about your future. Phones and films tend to be more exciting, more interesting, and less trouble.

Long gone are the times when people sat down and wrote letters in longhand or typed them on stationery, then put them in envelopes, added stamps, and carried them to the nearest mailbox or post office. Even e-mail is going out of style. Texting and phoning are beginning to supersede e-mail for quick communication, especially for young people.

Smart phones have opened up an even larger universe that already includes more apps than anyone can handle for everything from music and news to global positioning and systems for obeying oral commands. Embedded in all the new content is a new, rapidly changing language of acronyms, numbers, emoticons, and abbreviations that can be put into code for a closed group of people.

The bottom line is phoning is faster, easier, and more in style than writing or reading. And it is an excellent way to avoid being exposed to criticism for grammar and spelling.

A mobile phone can also help improve your overall image. Having one constantly on your ear in public tends to give you the appearance of being important and urgently involved with major decisions. You, too, can acquire such an image even though you may be merely telling your live-in what to get at the grocery store, listening to music, or getting a weather report.

Remember, with mobile phones, your image and handling of them may be more important than what you say or text on them.

LESSON THREE: FUDGE THE GRAMMAR

In order to become proficient in Amglish, you need to develop a nonchalant attitude toward grammar rules and standards. If English teachers themselves cannot always follow the rules of grammar, why should you even try?

That may mean forgetting much of what you have learned—or at least been exposed to—in school or at home. Although a certain basic knowledge is necessary, as it is in any language, you don't need to know the finer points.

Good grammar does not guarantee good communication. It can even be an impediment if it sets you apart from your peers.

Ambrose Bierce's *Devil's Dictionary* defines grammar as a "series of pitfalls thoughtfully prepared for the feet of the self-made man, along the path by which he advances to distinction."

Yet computer programs keep trying to improve grammar and syntax by inserting wavy lines under words and automatically changing the spelling of words when we try to innovate. The best way to handle such intrusions is to ignore them as much as possible.

To bond with others and be well understood, it is helpful to show that you yourself are far from perfect in the use of language. One way to do so is to downplay or avoid mysterious parts of English such as adverbs and subjunctives.

For leadership in this respect, let sports announcers and journalists be your guides. They tend to be on the cutting edge.

LESSON FOUR: BE CREATIVE WITH LANGUAGE

By buying or borrowing this book, you clearly show interest in enjoying language rather than being bored or agitated by it.

The word *Amglish* itself is an invention that invites other inventions in keeping with new ways of communicating. Amglish users are always looking for new words and new ways of saying things. This is one way to make more friends than you can on Facebook.

Newish words don't have to be instant successes. They don't even have to make sense to become popular, especially with young people, for whom new words are like basic foods for the ego. The only requirement is that words be original. We can't all be like Sarah in that respect, but there is no harm in trying.

If you cannot invent winning words, the next best thing is to pass on interesting ones you hear or see as promptly as possible. In this way, the cause of faster and livelier language can be further encouraged.

In fact, you can win prizes and gain prestige by entering one or more of the numerous word contests that are now the rage. One outlet is a dictionary that invites entries in an online daily word game. Just think of the fame, if not fortune, you may gain by dreaming up a word that becomes permanently enshrined in public discourse.

LESSON FIVE: ABBREVIATE WHERE POSSIBLE

In keeping with the basic aims of Amglish to save time and trouble, it is smart to shorten words and sentences as much as possible, except of course when you're on the phone and extra minutes don't cost much, or someone else is paying the bill. Keep an open mind for ways to be as brief and to the point as possible.

To begin with, make a detailed inventory of all the abbreviations you know and frequently review them so you will always be ready to insert them in all your writing and conversations. Your eventual acceptance in the extended Amglish family may depend not only on the extent of your verbal inventory but on your ability to use words freely, whether appropriately or not.

Take a lesson from the world of tweeting and texting. Learn how to say and write things with few words.

& don't limit yrself only to wll-known abbrs. You shd feel free to think up new ones 2 go long with old standbys. Rmembr: with new abbrs, it's not so much how suitbl they R but how orig they R, even if you are not sure they will B undrstd. And don't forget numbers 2, 4, and 8 for inserting into your writing. They can become big hits with parents and teachers.

You should also have an ample supply of acronyms ready for instant messages and e-mails.

LESSON SIX: LET WORDS SPELL THEMSELVES

Everyone knows that Microsoft Word and other software programs can help solve spelling problems with apps like spell-check.

If you misspell a word as you type, you may see it quickly and automatically corrected or see a wavy red line under the word, warning you that the letters are not correct. You can then guess what's wrong, but if you guess wrong, the red will linger a while and then die.

But automatic spellers are far from perfect, as earlier parts of this book have shown. The failure of the world's greatest minds to solve this common problem is further reason to let

words spell themselves. Automatic devices can sometimes make it worse than your own errors can.

The truth is that nobody is a perfect speller. And few people have the time to look up words in dictionaries, even online ones. It's easier to blame spell-check; it is designed to take a lot of abuse.

Misspelling has become so common that it, like selective grammar, is becoming a good-buddy badge, especially in the world of e-mailing and texting. The key is not to get uptight about spelling, because being meticulous in such language departments can lead to your being considered a nerd or worse by others.

One consolation: even Shakespeare had trouble spelling his own name.

LESSON SEVEN: DISCONNECT THE DOTS

Punctuation is another trip to the dark ages. Over the last four centuries, English has accumulated a hornet's nest of squiggly things that few people can figure out or put into their places with confidence, much less perfection.

The lesson here is like the first one: relax. Let your writing flow without restraint. Sentence breaks and breathing stops should come naturally. Problems occur when you have to choose which type of punctuation to use.

Let's start by separating the few necessary ones, such as commas and periods, from the ones that are rarely understood, such as colons and semicolons. From the looks of the word *semicolon*, it seems to be worth half a colon, but it's really only worth about a tenth of a colon. That means you should use the marks in that proportion.

Author and language expert Paul Robinson says that more than half the semicolons he sees "should be periods, and probably another quarter should be commas." He also says all punctuation should be "as invisible as possible" so as not to be a distraction.[1] One way to make them invisible is to use as few as possible.

On the other hand, famed nitpicker Lynne Truss admits that punctuation is going out of style.[2] Apparently all we need to do is to wait.

LESSON EIGHT: USE FILLERS, LIKE, A LOT

If you agree that it is time to slow down the language train so your thoughts can catch up to a conversation, this lesson is for you. It is about words you can nonchalantly mumble while you grab a split second or two to think about what you want—or don't want—to say next.

It should be clear by now that language changes are arriving much too fast for anyone to absorb or understand them all and still be able to respond smartly before the response gap becomes embarrassingly long.

When such a point arrives in a conversation, you have a wide choice of words or phrases—including some already well-known ones—that can give you those extra fractions of a second to plan your next words. There is no hiding the fact that the most-used fillers are *like* and *you know*.

The beauty of these handy words is that they are simply not noticed because almost everybody else uses them without realizing it or hearing themselves say them. The words can be inserted before, like, almost any other word or phrase without, you know, giving even a hint to people nearby that you are grasping for a more thoughtful response to what was said earlier.

Notice how the two types of pauses were slipped into the above sentence so deftly that they are not noticeable even in printed form.

After all, what are the alternatives? Who wants to hear a string of *ahs* and *uhs* or worse while waiting for the next word from a conversational partner?

LESSON NINE: KILL OBSCENITIES WITH EXCESS

As noted earlier, when Vice President Dick Cheney told Senator Patrick Leahy to "go f— yourself," the media reported it, but hardly anybody was shocked. Nor was anyone shocked when Vice President Joe Biden said the Obama health care bill was "a big f—ing deal."

Expletives and obscenities are still being used often, but some are clearly losing their punch because of overuse. The real killer here seems to be excessive repetition, not the pleas and threats of parents, teachers, or movie and broadcast codes.

Under the circumstances, the best way to strike a blow against the most offensive obscenities is to use them to excess until negative public reaction works its will.

Perhaps the best evidence for such an approach is the story (told earlier in this book) of what has happened to the verb *suck*, a word that often had an obscene meaning. Parents and teachers didn't kill its offensive meaning with threats. It died of natural causes from excessive use. More recently, it has even acquired respectability with a newly accepted meaning.

Meanwhile, the blogosphere has been inundated with obscenities. What sucks there is the anonymity. That seems to open the floodgates to obscenities galore.

LESSON TEN: LEARN TO CODE-SWITCH

Now for the real fun part: finding the tricky middle ground of language that allows you to shift lingos to fit the current scene, especially if you are young.

Professional linguists use the term code-switching (CS) to describe the ability to change from one type of language to another, such as changing from cool, street talk to the language necessary to get a college degree or a good job.

The initials of *code-switching* are the same as those for *cool smart*, the state of being able to know when to stop hanging with friends and when to learn enough of the prevailing language of media and business to achieve a happy and useful life.

We all code-switch to some extent to gain rapport with the person we are addressing at the moment. If it's a language teacher, we are likely to cut the street talk and show off a few big words. If it's a close friend or relative, we tend to revert to less formal terms.

As this book tries to make clear, language can be very enjoyable, especially with the informal lingo that is taking over the world and reshaping itself, as well as other languages, as it goes. But that doesn't mean you should not be proficient in the working language of society

Funny guy Bill Cosby is the model here. The TV comedian is not joking when he says he learned how to code-switch as a boy. He would use street slang with his playmates during the day, but when he got home and faced his homework, he shifted to the language that eventually helped him succeed beyond his fondest dreams.

In today's world of information technology (IT), people who can't handle both formal and informal language will sooner or later lose their way.

What makes all this especially exciting is that for the first time in history, one language seems to be well on the way to filling that need for much of the world.

Deciding to be *cool smart* is easy. The hard part is the follow-through.

Notes

MADE IN THE U.S.A.

1. Toni Boyle and K. D. Sullivan, *Gremlins of Grammar* (New York: Mc-Graw-Hill, 2006), p. 2.

2. *The New Republic*, April 6, 2011.

3. World-renowned linguist and author David Crystal has raised his estimate from 1.5 to 2.0 billion, the same figure used by David Graddol, another British authority on language. E-mail to author from Crystal, March 7, 2011.

4. Robert McCrum, *Globish* (New York: Norton, 2010), p. 276.

5. January 11, 2000.

6. November 6, 2000.

7. January 23, 2004.

8. April 11, 2001.

9. Simon Winchester, *The Professor and the Madman* (New York: HarperCollins, 1998), p. 242.

10. *Washington Post*, January 22, 2006.

11. November 22, 2006.

12. *Washington Post*, November 19, 2006.

13. Maureen Dowd, *New York Times*, July 25, 2007.

14. *Vanity Fair*, January 23, 2010.

15. *Washington Post*, December 23, 2007.

16. *Washington Post*, July 11, 2010.

17. Robert J. Connors and Andrea A. Lunsford, "Frequency of Formal Errors in Current College Writing, or Ma and Pa Kettle Do Research," *College Composition and Communication* 39 (December 1988): pp. 395–409; *The New St. Martin's Guide to Teaching Writing* (New York: Bedford/St. Martin's, 1993).

18. *Charlie Rose*, PBS, March 11, 2009.

19. E. D. Hirsch Jr., *The Knowledge Deficit* (Boston: Houghton Mifflin, 2006), p. 53.

20. *New Yorker*, June 18, 1949.

21. *Washington Post*, September 8, 2007.

22. Source: Denise T., the teacher.

23. http://teacherblue.homestead.com/penmanship.html.

24. Lynne Truss, *Eats, Shoots & Leaves* (New York: Gotham Books, 2008), p. 112.

25. Louis Menand, *New Yorker*, June 28, 2004.

26. David Spates, *Crossville Chronicle*, June 4, 2007.

27. *Highlights from PISA* (Program for International Student Assessment), U.S. Department of Education, National Center for Education Statistics, December 2010.

28. H. L. Mencken, *The American Language*, paperback ed. (New York: Knopf, 1977), p. 133.

29. Mencken, *The American Language*, p. 123.

30. http://www.mediamonitors.net/polatkaya1.html.

TEACHERS AND OTHER PIONEERS

1. The full sentence from the NCTE statement is, "In view of the widespread agreement of research studies based upon many types of students and teachers, the conclusion can be stated in strong and unqualified terms: the teaching of formal grammar has a negligible or, because it usually displaces some instruction and practice in composition, even a harmful effect on the improvement of writing."

2. Telephone conversation, February 19, 2007.

3. Edwin C. Newman, *Strictly Speaking: Will America Be the Death of English?* (Brunswick, NJ: Transaction Publishers, 1974).

4. John Algeo, PBS, *Do You Speak American?* Language Myth No. 21, 2005.

5. *Mail Online*, January 21, 2010.

6. David Mulroy, *The War against Grammar* (Portsmouth, NH: Heinemann-Boynton/Cook, 2003).

7. *New York Times*, November 11, 1993.

8. United Press International, October 22, 2010.

9. *Guardian*, February 4, 2005.

10. *Yahoo! Answers*, August 31, 2010.

11. www.gettingpastgo.org/docs/Literature-Review-GPG.pdf.

12. Sandra Stotsky, *Losing Our Language* (San Francisco: Free Press, 1999).

13. Diane Ravitch, *Language Police* (New York: Knopf, 2003).

14. Wolf Larsen, *Dana Society Journal*, February 2000.

15. John Bassett McCleary, *Hippie Dictionary* (Berkeley, CA: Ten Speed Press, 2002), p. xi.

16. *Online News Hour*, December 8, 2003.

17. Paul Dickson, *Family Words* (Oak Park, IL: Marion Street Press, 2007).

18. *Roth v. United States*, 354 U.S. 476 (1957).

19. *Washington Post*, April 25, 2007.

20. *Washington Post*, April 25, 2007.

21. Associated Press, January 4, 2011.

22. *FCC v. Pacifica Foundation*, 1978.

23. Mencken, *The American Language*, p. 85.

24. Mencken, *The American Language*, p. 80.

25. Associated Press, January 5, 2011.

THE NEW WORLD LINGO

1. *Daily Mail*, February 27, 2006.

2. William Shakespeare, *Henry V*, 5.11.235.

3. Hendrik Kasimir, *Haphazard Reality* (New York: Harper & Row, 1984).

4. http://adaniel.tripod.com/india.htm.

5. Sidney J. Baker, "The Influence of American Slang on Australia," *American Speech*, American Dialect Society, December 1943.

6. Lane Crothers, *Globalization & American Popular Culture* (Lanham, MD: Rowman & Littlefield, 2010), p. 183.

7. Paul Z. Jambor, "English Language Imperialism," *Journal of English as an International Language* 2 (December 2007): p. 197.

8. E-mail to author, January 17, 2011.

9. Lois Beckwith, *The Dictionary of Corporate Bullshit* (New York: Broadway Brooks, 2006).

10. J. Hornikx, F. Van Meurs, and A. de Boer, "English or Local Advertising?" *Journal of Business Communication* 47, no. 2 (2010): pp. 169–88.

11. E-mail to author, April 16, 2011.

12. "English in a Changing World," *Association Internationale de Linguistique Appliquee*, Review 13, 1999.

13. "Goodbye My Blind Majesty," in *Global Pop, Local Language*, ed. Harris M. Berger and Michael T. Carroll (Jackson: University Press of Mississippi, 2003), p. 53–86.

14. Jamie Shinhee Lee, "Language and Identity: Entertainers in South Korean Pop Culture," in *Identity and Second Language Learning*, ed. Miguel Mantero (Charlotte, NC: Information Age, 2007), pp. 283–303.

15. PBS, *Do You Speak American?* September 28, 2005.

16. Braj Kachru, *The Alchemy of English* (Oxford: Pergamon Press, 1986), p. 1.

17. Kachru, *The Alchemy of English*, p. 145.

18. Ahmet Acar and Paul Robertson, *English as an International Language Journal* 5 (2009): p. 25.

19. www.eltnewsletter.com/back/May2002/art992002.htm.

20. *Christian Science Monitor*, May 16, 1995.

21. Juliane House, *Guardian Weekly*, April 19, 2001.

22. *New York Times*, April 25, 2010.

23. E-mail to author, February 20, 2011.

24. *Daily Mail Online*, March 12, 2008.

25. *Daily Mail Online*, April 25, 2010.

26. E-mail to author, January 17, 2011.

27. *Atlantic Times*, November 2006.

28. John H. McWhorter, *The Power of Babel* (New York: HarperCollins, 2001), p. 117.

29. Peter Beattie, *AustralianPolitics.com*, March 10, 2003.

30. *American Speech* 18, no. 4 (December 1943): pp. 253–56.

31. *U.S.-China Education Review* 4, no. 5 (May 2007).

32. Paul J. Jambor, "English Language Imperialism," *Journal of English as an International Language* 2 (December 2007): p. 104.

33. http://beingLatino.wordpress.com/2010/05/04/what-in-the-heights-means-to-us.

34. *Barcelona Review*, January–February 2004.

35. BBC, December 21, 2010.

36. http://www.youtube.com/watch?v=cvtWAXoZjTc.

37. E-mail to author, December 2, 2010.

38. *Slovak Spectator*, April 5, 2010.

39. *New York Times*, July 26, 2010.

40. July 29, 2004.

41. Salman Rushdie, *Imaginary Homelands* (London: Granta Books, 1991).

42. *Henry Stewart Publications* 1 (2003): pp. 129–149.

43. Richard Gibson, *Wall Street Journal*, August 11, 2009.

44. Nicholas Ostler, *The Last Lingua Franca* (New York: Walker Publishing, 2010).

45. David Graddol, "The Future of Language," *Science*, February 27, 2004.

46. David Crystal, *The Stories of English* (London: Penguin, 2004).

47. *New York Times*, December 11, 2010.

48. *New York Times*, August 19, 2010.

FROM REVOLUTION TO TSUNAMI

1. May 10, 2000.

2. Ilan Stavans, *Spanglish* (New York: Harper Perennial, 2003), p. 2.

3. *London Telegraph*, March 24, 2010.

4. James Boswell, *The Life of Samuel Johnson*, paperback ed. (New York: Penguin, [1791] 2008), p. 277.

5. Lewis Thomas, *The Lives of a Cell: Notes of a Biology Watcher* (New York: Viking, 1974), p. 46.

6. Leslie Dunton-Downer, *The English Is Coming* (New York: Simon & Schuster, 2010).

7. *Economist*, November 11, 2010.

8. William Powers, *Hamlet's Blackberry* (New York: HarperCollins, 2010), p. 40.

9. CBS News, February 15, 2010.

10. November 24, 2010.

11. "Nokia Taking a Rural Road to Growth," *New York Times*, November 1, 2010.

12. Interview, December 10, 2010.

13. *New York Times*, November 11, 2010.

14. *Discover Magazine*, June 18, 2009.

15. *London Telegraph*, August 6, 2009.

16. Norman Silver, *Age, Sex, Location* (Colchester: tXt café, 2006).

17. *New York Times*, November 10, 2010.

18. Bob Hirschfeld, *Washington Post*, September 26, 2009.

19. *Washington Post*, June 15, 2008.

20. *Washington Post*, June 15, 2008.

21. *New York Times*, November 21, 2010.

22. Robin Dunbar, *The Origin and Subsequent Evolution of Language* (New York: Oxford University Press, 2004).

23. David Crystal, *The Language Revolution* (Malden, MA: Polity Press, 2004), p. 4.

24. E-mail to author, March 17, 2007.

25. *New York Times*, July 2, 2010.

26. *New York Times*, December 8, 2010.

27. Jean-Luc Nancy's open letter, *New York Times*, December 5, 2010.

28. Michael Parkvall, *Limits of Language* (Wilsonville, OR: William, James & Co., 2008), p. 23.

29. Robert McCrum, *Globish* (New York: Norton, 2010), p. 285.

THE LISHES OF AMGLISH

1. Jug Suraiaya, *Times of India*, June 13, 1999.

2. Tony Badran, phone interview, February 22, 2011.

3. *New York Times*, May 3, 2010.

4. *Journal of Pragmatics* 41, no. 6 (June 2009): pp. 1139–51.

5. E-mails to author, January 23–26, 2011.

6. http://netmesh.info/jernst/comments/yet-more-germanglish.

7. http://wtforum.nl/forum/showthread.php?t=5018.

8. E-mail from Monique Briendwalker.

9. *Korea Times*, June 5, 2007.

10. E-mail to author from Maria Angela Loguercio Bouskela.

11. E-mail to author, October 13, 2005.

12. http://en.wikipedia.org/wiki/Runglish.

13. E-mail to author from Feodor Bratenkov.

14. E-mail to author, February 15, 2011.

TEN EASY LESSONS

1. *New Republic*, April 26, 1980.

2. Truss, *Eats, Shoots & Leaves*, p. 112.

Index